INSIDE YOUR ANNUAL 2021!

D0246919

BUILD YOUR DREAM XI 40

10 REASONS TO BE BUZZING FOR... EURO 2020!

EURO 2020 PREVIEW 18

F2
BECOMING YOUTUBE LEGENDS!

THE F2 INTERVIEW 68

THE G.O.A.Ts

STRIKERS

G.O.A.T. STRIKERS 88

100 PREMIER LEAGUE GOALS CLUB

100 PREM GOAL CLUB 80

This time last year we were well buzzing about football in 2020, but it got totally derailed! We're hoping that 2021 will make up for it – here's what we're most looking forward to...

NEW ERA

Cristiano Ronaldo and Lionel Messi have dominated footy for over a decade, but their time is coming to an end! In 2021 we could see them replaced at the top of the game by younger stars like Jadon Sancho, Kylian Mbappe and Erling Haaland! Could one of them bag the Ballon d'Or?

FOOTBALL'S COMING BACK!

OLYMPICS

In July, straight after the Euros, teams will head to Tokyo aiming to win gold at the Olympics! Brazil are the holders of the men's tournament after winning on home soil in 2016, while Team GB will be aiming to become the first British side to bag a footy medal since 1912 in the women's competition!

CHECK OUT OUR EURO 2020 PREVIEW ON PAGE 18!

EUROS TAKE TWO

We were gutted when the Euros got pushed back a year, but at least we've got a wicked competition to look forward to next summer! There are plenty of young stars that'll be ready to tear up the comp with an extra season's experience - like Mason Greenwood, Bukayo Saka and Phil Foden - while players and fans will want to make the most of the tournament big time after its postponement!

EPIC ATMOSPHERES

Watching so much footy behind closed doors in 2020 has been heartbreaking – the game is nothing without the fans! We want to see supporters going nuts in the stands every single week in 2021, with the biggest games in the Prem, Champions League and cups played out in front of sold-out stadiums. Fingers crossed!

WSL

2020 was a horrible year for the WSL too, with Chelsea awarded the title after the season ended early. We want to see the league return to full strength in the New Year, with some of the best talents in the women's game at the peak of their powers battling to lift next season's title!

WE'VE PICKED TEN WOMEN'S PLAYERS TO WATCH AT THE OLYMPICS ON PAGE 22!

INTERNATIONAL FOOTY IN 2021!

The football calendar was messed up in 2020, but 2021 should more than make up for it! Check out the tournaments that are set to take place...

EURO 2020
June 11–July 11

As planned last year to celebrate the European Championship's 60th anniversary, 12 host cities will stage the matches – including London and Glasgow!

COPA AMERICA
June 11–July 11

Like the Euros, South America's major footy comp got pushed back a year. Argentina and Colombia will be sharing hosting duties!

GOLD CUP
July 2-25

The men's senior international tournaments will be rounded off by CONCACAF's major competition – the 16th in its history – with Mexico aiming for a record ninth title!

OLYMPICS
July 21-August 7

Both the men and women's events will be packed with quality, but Team GB are only sending a female team to Tokyo!

RONALDO'S RECORDS

In 2020, Cristiano Ronaldo marked the 1,000th game of his career by scoring his 725th goal! Although he's well into his 30s, the Portugal legend still has loads left in his locker, so MATCH checks out the records he wants to break next...

11
CR7 will go to next summer's Euros level with Cesc Fabregas and Andres Iniesta for most Euro matches won – 11! He only needs one more win to set a new record!

150
Ronaldo's battled with Lionel Messi for the CL goal record for years, but now he's well ahead of the Barca legend. He could be the first player to reach 150!

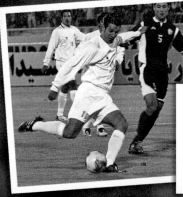

109
He was stuck on 99 international goals before lockdown. After scoring his 100th goal, his next target will be Iran legend Ali Daei's all-time record of 109!

9
He's also level with France legend Michel Platini for most goals scored at the Euros on nine, so he'll surely set a new record for that as well!

TOP 5...
FASTEST PREM GOALS!

1	2	3	4	5

Shane Long	**Ledley King**	**Alan Shearer**	**Christian Eriksen**	**Mark Viduka**
Watford v Southampton	Bradford v Tottenham	Newcastle v Man. City	Tottenham v Man. United	Charlton v Leeds
7.69 seconds	*9.82 seconds*	*10.52 seconds*	*10.54 seconds*	*11.90 seconds*

5

Euro 2020 will be the fifth Euros of Ronaldo's career – more than any other player – and he's scored at each of the last four!

6

Cristiano is one of ten players who's won the Champions League five times – he's only one behind Paco Gento's all-time record!

177

Legendary keeper Iker Casillas has the record for most Champions League appearances, but CR7 can catch him in 2021!

1000

Ronaldo wants to end his career with over 1,000 goals! In the last five years, he's scored well over 200 for club and country, so if he carries on at that rate he'll have to play into his 40s to reach the landmark!

3

One more CL victory will also take him level with Clarence Seedorf's record of lifting the trophy with three different clubs!

CROSSING THE DIVIDE!

Check out the players that got fans raging by moving from one huge rival to another!

LUIS FIGO
2000: BARCELONA TO REAL MADRID

Barca fans were so angry with Figo for joining Real, one of them threw a pig's head at him on his next visit to the Nou Camp!

SOL CAMPBELL
2001: TOTTENHAM TO ARSENAL

Campbell left Spurs to join their North London rivals, and ended up winning the title at White Hart Lane with The Gunners. Ouch!

ASHLEY COLE
2006: ARSENAL TO CHELSEA

Chelsea got in big trouble for speaking to Cole without Arsenal's permission in 2005, but he still moved a year later!

CARLOS TEVEZ
2009: MAN. UNITED TO MAN. CITY

When Tevez's move across Manchester was confirmed, City unfurled a huge 'Welcome To Manchester' banner to wind up United!

MATTY TAYLOR
2017: BRISTOL ROVERS TO BRISTOL CITY

City exploited a contract clause to snap up their local rivals' top goalscorer on deadline day in January 2017!

DID YOU KNOW?

Brazil and Sao Paulo legend Rogerio Ceni is the highest-scoring goalkeeper of all time! He bagged over 131 goals in his career thanks to his wicked free-kick and penalty-taking tekkers!

2020'S WEIRDEST BANNER

Remember when fans of Dutch side ADO Den Haag celebrated the arrival of Alan Pardew and his assistant Chris Powell with this massive Ghostbusters banner? Well Random!

QUICK QUIZ! In 2020 Liverpool became the seventh club to win the Premier League title! Can you name the other six?

Turn over for answers!

FOOTBALL FIGHTS BACK!

MATCH looks back on 2020, and how the football family united to fight back against Coronavirus and footy being locked down!

#STAYATHOMECHALLENGE!

There were loads of different #StayAtHomeChallenges to keep the stars and public entertained during lockdown! The one that really seemed to kick it all off in the footy world was kick-ups with a toilet roll! The likes of Lionel Messi, Marcus Rashford, Joao Felix, Tammy Abraham and Vinicius Junior all got involved. Quality!

EPREMIER LEAGUE INVITATIONALS!

INVITATIONAL CHAMPION
JAMES MADDISON

INVITATIONAL CHAMPION

Prem superstars put their FIFA skills to the test in two FIFA 20 tournaments, with the prize funds being donated to the #PlayersTogether initiative – a way for stars to generate money for the NHS! Wolves' Diogo Jota edged out Trent Alexander-Arnold 2-1 in the first final, while James Maddison won the second edition!

FRIDAY FAMILY CHALLENGE!

Every Friday during lockdown, the Premier League and Premier League Communities put out a Family Challenge with different tasks for households to try to complete – including writing letters and poems, plus solving maths problems! How many did your family take on?

Premier League
QUICK QUIZ ANSWERS!
These teams have all won the Premier League in the past. Did you guess all six correctly?

Man. United		Chelsea	
Blackburn		Man. City	
Arsenal		Leicester	

STADIUM WATCH!

The 2021 Champions League final will be at Istanbul's Ataturk Olympic Stadium – the venue that hosted Liverpool's mad 2005 CL final comeback against AC Milan! It was originally supposed to host the 2020 CL final, before getting moved to Lisbon!

DID YOU KNOW?

1857 SHEFFIELD F.C.
THE WORLD'S FIRST FOOTBALL CLUB

The oldest football club in the world is Sheffield FC! The club currently plays footy in the Northern Premier League Division One South East, and in 2021 they'll celebrate their 164th birthday!

GENEROUS GROUNDS!

Loads of top-flight clubs virtually handed over their stadiums to the NHS to help battle Coronavirus. Chelsea allowed use of their Stamford Bridge hotel to NHS staff, Tottenham and Brighton's stadiums were used as drive-thru testing centres, while nurses took training courses at Man. City's Etihad Stadium!

FAN SURPRISE

PRESENTED BY

MAKING A DIFFERENCE!

Loads of players used their extra time and profile to make a difference to society during the pandemic. Ballers Juan Mata and James Maddison made video calls to supporters in isolation to give them a lift, while Marcus Rashford joined forces with FareShare to campaign for access to free school meals, causing a U-turn in UK government policy!

James Maddison — Roy Fellows

MATCH! ON SOCIAL!

MATCH had loads of social media campaigns to keep our followers entertained while footy was on hold as well!

#MYMATCHSHIRT

We posted some wacky shirts from our collection, and asked readers to send in their favourite football jerseys too!

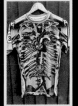

#MATCHSOCKUPS

The Knuckleball Twins, freestyler Ben Nuttall and Man. United women star Ella Toone all got involved in our scrunched sock-ups challenge. Class!

#MATCHKICKUPS

MATCH also had a more normal kick-ups challenge, with one of our followers managing over 200! Top tekkers!

#MATCHULTIMATEPLAYER

Hundreds of our followers voted to create an Ultimate Player with current superstars, and then we asked people to draw what it'd look like!

TEKKERS TIPS!

StayAtHome SKILLS ACADEMY BY BEN NUTTALL

Everyone was forced to work from home, but clubs made it easier by posting fun footy challenges! Chelsea uploaded drills to YouTube on how to improve your technique, Everton had a series of Garden Skills to learn, and Liverpool got fans to recreate famous goals! Footy freestyler Ben Nuttall also helped out with step-by-step videos on how to complete different tricks!

FOOTY FLASHBACK

Back in the 2017 MATCH Annual, we took a shot at guessing how England would line up at Euro 2020! How close do you think we'll be?

ENGLAND'S FUTURE XI!

RECORD CHASERS

If Celtic win the Scottish Premiership in 2020-21, they'll be the first side in history to win the trophy ten times in a row! Both Rangers and Celtic have won nine on the trot before, but never reached double figures!

GAFFER GAFFE!

The social media slip-up of the year has to go to Cincinnati FC! After they announced ex-Man. United hero Jaap Stam as their new manager in May, they revealed the news with a pic of Ajax youth coach Tinus van Teunenbroek instead. EPIC FAIL!

IT'S A BIG YEAR FOR...

MASON GREENWOOD
Man. United & England

Last season was a real breakout year for the teenage sensation - he hit 17 goals in all comps - but we think 2021 will be an even bigger year for Mason! If the two-footed goal king continues his progress and keeps hammering in the goals, it'll be hard to keep him out of England's starting line-up at the European Championship!

LAUTARO MARTINEZ
Inter & Argentina

Argentina haven't been short of attacking talent over the last 28 years, but they haven't won the Copa America since 1993! Their latest world-class striker could make the difference after tearing up Serie A - especially if he joins Barcelona to form a lethal partnership with his international skipper Lionel Messi!

EDEN HAZARD
Real Madrid & Belgium

Hazard's first year in Spain didn't go to plan after it was wrecked by injury, but he still got his hands on the La Liga title! The winger needs to start repaying his £89m fee with some big displays before heading to the Euros, where Belgium will be one of the hot faves. If the dribbler's on form, Real and Belgium could be unstoppable!

TREND SETTERS

Meet the legends that invented footy's most famous tricks...

CRUYFF TURN

Now it's one of the most common moves in footy, but defenders were baffled by it when Johan Cruyff started busting out his famous turn!

ELASTICO

Also known as the flip-flap, this move was born in Brazil! Ronaldinho was sick at it, but it was actually invented by legendary winger Rivelino in the 1960s and '70s!

MEMPHIS DEPAY
Lyon & Netherlands

Nobody benefitted from the Euros being postponed more than Depay. He fired Netherlands to the tournament with six goals and seven assists in qualifying, but then got ruled out of the finals by a knee injury! Now that he's got a second chance, he'll be desperate to fire The Oranje to glory!

RICHARLISON
Everton & Brazil

Gossips say Everton turned down an £85 million offer from Barcelona for Richarlison in 2019! In 2021 he'll turn 24 and hit his full potential and, if he keeps improving, his value will only get higher. Everton could struggle to hold onto him, especially if he helps fire Brazil to Copa America success, just like he did in 2019!

PHIL FODEN
Man. City & England

Pep Guardiola has described Foden as the best young talent he's worked with - and this year he has the chance to prove it! David Silva's exit means there's a space in Man. City's midfield for the wonderkid, and if he hits his potential then he should be in Gareth Southgate's plans for the Euros too!

FOOTY FAMILIES!

Check out the stars following in their father's footsteps!

GIOVANNI REYNA

Gio was born in Sunderland while his dad **CLAUDIO** played in the Prem, so the Dortmund wonderkid could play for USA or England!

MARCOS LLORENTE

The Atletico Madrid midfielder's dad, uncle and grandfather all played for Real Madrid, while his great uncle was the legendary **PACO GENTO**!

IANIS HAGI

The skilful Rangers attacking midfielder is the son of Romania's greatest-ever player - ex-Real Madrid and Barcelona superstar **GHEORGHE**!

MATTHEUS OLIVEIRA

Ex-Brazil striker **BEBETO** celebrated the birth of his son at World Cup '94 with his 'cradle-rocking' celebration - and now he's a pro player himself at Sporting!

GOAL MACHINE ERLING HAALAND IS THE SON OF A FOOTBALLER TOO! FIND OUT MORE ABOUT HIM ON PAGE 28!

PANENKA PENALTY

At Euro '76, Czech striker Antonin Panenka fooled the GK by faking to blast a penalty, before dinking it instead! That's why the move is named after him!

RABONA

Neymar is the master of it now, but footy historians reckon Argentina striker Ricardo Infante was the first player to pull off a rabona in the 1940s!

MARSEILLE ROULETTE

The 360° spinning move was mastered by legends Zinedine Zidane and Diego Maradona, but started with French striker Yves Mariot the 1970s!

WIN!

EPOS SENNHEISER GSP 300 GAMING HEADSET!

TOTTENHAM
HOTSPUR

LEGENDS

2020

KANE

THE G.O.A.Ts

Lev Yashin
1950-1970
Country: Russia

Main Clubs: Dynamo Moscow

GOAT Credentials: The only goalkeeper to win the Ballon d'Or, Yashin totally changed how the position was played. He was one of the first GKs to dominate his penalty area, and his displays took Russia to an Olympic gold medal in 1956 and the first-ever Euros in 1960! He was so good, the award for the World Cup's best GK is named after him!

Gordon Banks
1958-1977
Country: England

Main Clubs: Leicester, Stoke

GOAT Credentials: If you look up the greatest saves ever made, you'll see Banks' name. At the 1970 World Cup, the England legend produced an epic stop to keep out a header from Brazil superstar Pele! He was named FIFA's GK Of The Year five times in a row, starting in 1966 when he was in nets for England's only World Cup victory!

GOALKEEPERS

We're starting our look back over football's all-time greats with the goalkeepers! These heroes were almost unbeatable in their prime!

Oliver Kahn
1987-2008
Country: Germany

Main Clubs: Karlsruher, Bayern Munich

GOAT Credentials: Kahn's displays at the 2002 World Cup were good enough to take Germany all the way to the final and made him the first goalkeeper in history to win the Golden Ball! He also won more games and kept more clean sheets than any player in Bundesliga history, and helped Bayern win the Champo League and eight league titles in 11 years!

Peter Schmeichel
1981-2003
Country: Denmark

Main Clubs: Brondby, Man. United

GOAT Credentials: The Great Dane starred in the Denmark side that won Euro '92, then lifted five PL titles with Man. United, including their 1999 treble season! He was known for filling his goal and dominating his penalty area, and regularly came out on top in one-on-ones with strikers!

HONOURABLE MENTIONS

Dino Zoff

Sepp Maier

Pat Jennings

Petr Cech

David Seaman

Peter Shilton

Edwin van der Sar

Iker Casillas
1998-2020

Country: Spain

Main Clubs: Real Madrid, Porto

GOAT Credentials: Casillas spent his entire career at the top of the game. He was a Champo League winner at the age of 19, and went on to win the competition two more times and make a record 177 appearances! His international career was even better - he captained Spain to back-to-back European Championships and the World Cup, conceding just six goals in the process. Wow!

DID YOU KNOW?

In Spain's victories at Euro 2008, Euro 2012 and the 2010 World Cup, Casillas kept a clean sheet in every single one of the nation's knockout-stage games!

PRETENDERS

These stars will enter the GOAT conversation when they eventually retire!

David De Gea
Man. United & Spain

De Gea has been pulling off incredible saves for years, and will definitely go down as one of the best shot-stoppers of all time in the Premier League!

Gianluigi Buffon
Juventus & Italy

Nobody has played more games, won more titles or kept more clean sheets in Serie A than the Italy and Juventus legend – and he's still going strong aged 42!

Manuel Neuer
Bayern Munich & Germany

As well as being a solid goalie, Neuer is like an extra outfield player - the sweeper keeper's rapid off his line and is mega comfortable with the ball at his feet!

Jan Oblak
Atletico Madrid & Slovenia

Since moving to Spain from Portugal in 2014, Oblak has made saves for fun, kept tons of cleans sheets and won the Zamora Trophy four times in a row!

Alisson
Liverpool & Brazil

In the last few years Alisson has helped make Liverpool the champions of the world, Europe and Premier League, and Brazil champions of South America!

Thibaut Courtois
Real Madrid & Belgium

Undisputed Belgium No.1 Courtois is a giant that fills the goal and dominates his six-yard box - that's why he's won league titles in England and Spain!

EURO 2020

... WHAT WOULD HAVE HAPPENED!

We were gutted when Euro 2020 got postponed for a year, so we've imagined what happened instead!

WAKE ME FROM THIS NIGHTMARE, MATCH!

MY BARBER'S IN MASSIVE TROUBLE!

RONALDO'S RECORDS RUINED!

Cristiano Ronaldo went to the Euros chasing loads of records! He became the first player to appear at five European Championships, then broke Michel Platini's all-time scoring record! His bid to become the second captain to lift back-to-back trophies fell apart, though – 16 years after scoring in a shootout v England, The Three Lions beat Portugal in the final on penalties!

POGBA'S BARNET MIX-UP!

Paul Pogba marked the epic tournament in typical style by dying his hair in the colours of the French flag, but during the group games the white section turned yellow. That was pretty awkward for their knockout tie v Romania, because he ended up with their flag's colours on his head instead. Oops!

THEY ALL COUNT, DON'T THEY?

KANE'S FLUKEY GOLDEN BOOT!

Cristiano Ronaldo's new goal record lasted a matter of days before Harry Kane broke it! The England skipper scored 11 goals to fire The Three Lions to the trophy, including seven penalties, a one-yard tap-in, two over-hit crosses and a rocket Marcus Rashford shot that deflected in off Kane's backside!

WALES, GOLF, MADRID!

Wales followed their Euro 2016 heroics with another memorable tournament – but Gareth Bale's relationship with Real Madrid was damaged beyond repair. After banging in a free-kick to knock Spain out of the quarter-finals, the winger and his team-mates brought out this infamous flag again!

KDB: ASSIST MACHINE!

Belgium were the top-scoring nation in the tournament by far, thanks to one man. They scored 15 goals in the group stage, and Kevin De Bruyne set up every single one of them! By the end of the Euros, the Man. City star had broken every assist record in the book with a total of 20!

ON A PLATE AGAIN!

NO ONE GETS PAST ME!

YOU'LL NEVER BEAT VAN DIJK!

Virgil van Dijk made it through the Premier League season with hardly any attacker dribbling past him, but his Euros record was even better. The Netherlands defender found it so easy against opposition forwards, he ditched his boots and switched to slippers for the knockout stages!

MAYOR OF LONDON!

Germany's run to the semi-finals took Serge Gnabry to London for the third time that season after Champions League clashes at Spurs and then Chelsea. With a freshly-grown Afro, the Bayern Munich winger banged in a hat-trick past Hugo Lloris in the France goal, to make it nine goals in three visits to the capital!

EAT MY DUST, PAL!

YOU GOTTA BE KIDDING ME!

CAN I PLAY HERE EVERY WEEK?

USAIN MBAPPE!

After burning past defenders all summer for Les Bleus, Kylian Mbappe completed an unlikely transfer. When France's athletics team were struck down by injuries, they snapped up the PSG star for the Tokyo Olympics straight after the competition, and he picked up a gold medal in the 100 metres final and silver in the relay!

10 REASONS TO BE BUZZING FOR... EURO 2020!

Even though it's taking place in the summer of 2021, the next Euros will still be known as EURO 2020 to honour the original event – and MATCH is totally pumped up for it! Here are ten reasons why...

1

LONG WAIT!

The whole continent was mega motivated for last summer's epic tournament, but we all know what happened instead. The fact that we missed out on a major international tourno makes us even more excited for this year's event. They say good things come to those who wait, so it should be a cracker!

2

CLASS CEREMONIES!

Major football events always have wicked opening and closing ceremonies - world-famous DJ David Guetta performed at the start and end of Euro 2016 in France! We're expecting some top tekkers, at the very least – mega mascot Skillzy is a freestyle expert, and he'll perform some tricks alongside co-mascots Tobias Becs and Liv Cooke!

SICK CELEBRATIONS!

For some reason, the biggest stars love doing new and crazy celebrations at international tournaments! At World Cup 2018, it was all about Fortnite - Antoine Griezmann busted out the 'Take The L', Jesse Lingard did the 'Hype' dance and Dele Alli did the 'Ride The Pony'! Which trend will take over this time?

3

FOOTY FESTIVAL!

Just as originally planned, the competition will be spread across 12 different countries for the first time in its history, so there's going to be a party atmosphere all across the continent! That means country flags hanging from car windows, people getting together to watch the games and wacky fans dressed up in mega crazy costumes!

4

GOLDEN BOOT BATTLE!

At every Euros and World Cup, the planet's deadliest goal grabbers battle it out for the Golden Boot! Harry Kane will be looking to build on his collection after winning the World Cup 2018 prize, Antoine Griezmann will be hoping for back-to-back Euro wins, while Robert Lewandowski, Kylian Mbappe and Romelu Lukaku are also in the mix!

5

UPSETS ALERT!

Every nation has earned its spot for these Euros - there wasn't a free ticket for the hosts like in previous tournaments! That means it'll be a wide-open competition, so expect some big shocks - like when Iceland knocked out England in the last 16 of Euro 2016, or when outsiders Greece lifted the trophy way back in 2004!

6

7

CR7'S RECORD CHASE!

Cristiano Ronaldo will be 36 years old at the Euros, but he's on a record-breaking mission - he's just one goal away from becoming the outright top goalscorer in European Championship history! He's also not far away from becoming the highest international scorer in men's footy - Iran's Ali Daei is currently top on 109!

TRANSFER TARGETS!

Even though the Euros takes place in one continent, fans and scouts all across the world will be tuning into the action! Massive names and potential wonderkids see it as a window of opportunity to showcase their top talent - and maybe earn themselves a big-money move! We can't wait to see which stars shine in 2021!

8

9

GROUP OF DEATH!

We already know the groups for next summer's tournament, and we've got our eyes firmly locked on Group F - mega nations Portugal, France and Germany are competing for the top two spots! Keep an eye out for England's clash with Croatia, too - the Group D match is a repeat of the 2018 World Cup semi-final!

10

FOOTY'S COMING HOME!

We've already mentioned that matches will be played across 12 cities and 12 stadiums, but only one will host the semi-finals and final - and that's Wembley! It's a great opportunity for England to gain some home advantage but, even if The Three Lions fall at an earlier hurdle, the nation will still get to stage a major international final!

TURN OVER FOR OUR EURO 2020 BOARD GAME!

WIN THE EUROS!

Can you go all the way from the group stage to the European Championship final? Use some coins as counters, grab a dice and battle your friends and family in this epic football board game!

START ▶
KICK-OFF!
The player who rolls the highest number goes first!

2 ▶

3 ▶
LEGEND! You're named in your country's final 23-man squad! Move forward three spaces!

4 ▶

5 ▶
FAIL! You trip up at the opening ceremony and become a meme! Move back a space!

6 ▶

◀ 12
FAIL! A terrible Twitter gaffe gets you some negative headlines! Move back a space!

◀ 11

◀ 10
FAIL! You get a red card for a shocking flying tackle! Move back four spaces!

◀ 9

◀ 8
LEGEND! You score the tournament's opening goal! Move forward three spaces!

◀ 7

13 ▶

14 ▶
LEGEND! Your group-stage displays impress scouts at some big Champions League clubs! Move forward two spaces!

15 ▶
FAIL! Cristiano Ronaldo says you're 'well overrated'! Move back two spaces!

16 ▶

17 ▶
FAIL! You miss a penalty in the round of 16 after a 20-step run-up! Move back four spaces!

18 ▶
LEGEND! An overhead kick sees your side qualify for the quarter-finals! Move forward four spaces!

◀ 24
LEGEND! You score a backheeled winner to go through to the semi-finals! Move forward two spaces!

◀ 23

◀ 22

◀ 21
LEGEND! You get a massive interview and poster in MATCH! Move forward two spaces!

◀ 20
FAIL! You're involved in a huge training-ground bust-up and get fined! Move back one space!

◀ 19

25 ▶
FAIL! You react badly to getting subbed off and lose some fans' respect! Move back three spaces!

26 ▶

27 ▶
LEGEND! Your cool goal celebration gets featured on the MATCH Instagram channel and goes viral! Move forward four spaces!

28 ▶

29 ▶
FAIL! The manager tells you you're not training hard enough! Move back six spaces!

30 ▶
LEGEND! Shirts with your name on the back sell out! Move forward one space!

◀ 36

◀ 35
LEGEND! You hit a hat-trick in the semis to fire your side into the final! Move forward three spaces!

◀ 34
FAIL! You're caught sneaking a take-away into the hotel! Move back three spaces!

◀ 33

◀ 32
FAIL! A horror haircut sees you lose your mega cool locks! Move back four spaces!

◀ 31

37 ▶
LEGEND! You're named as captain for the Euros final! Move forward three spaces!

38 ▶

39 ▶
FAIL! You get injured and are told you're a doubt for the final! Move back six spaces!

40 ▶

41 ▶
FAIL! You miss an absolute sitter in the Euros final! Move back three spaces!

WINNER!
YOU'RE A FOOTY LEGEND! YOU'VE WON THE EUROS!

LEGENDS

2020

AUBAMEYANG

10 STARS TO WATCH
...AT THE FOOTY OLYMPICS!

We'll be cheering on Great Britain in the summer of 2021 at the women's football tournament in Tokyo 2020, but we'll want to catch a glimpse of these stars too!

MEGAN RAPINOE
USA

Rapinoe ruled the 2019 World Cup, but her last Olympic Games was less successful. She came off the bench during the quarter-final with Sweden, but only lasted 27 minutes before being hooked off, with USA going on to lose on penalties! She'll be desperate to recapture the form that helped her win a gold medal in 2012!

CHRISTINE SINCLAIR
Canada

With more international goals than any other player in history and almost 300 caps, Sinclair is one of the all-time greats of women's footy! She's fired Canada to bronze medals at the last two Olympics, winning the Golden Boot in 2012, but she's still waiting for her first major international trophy. Can she end that wait in Tokyo?

MANA IWABUCHI
Japan

This will be Japan's first Olympic Games since 2012, when they bagged a silver medal after losing to USA in the final. If they're going to pick up another medal, they'll need Iwabuchi at her best - she was named MVP on the way to winning the Asia Cup in 2018, then starred at the World Cup too. If she's on form, the hosts have a great chance!

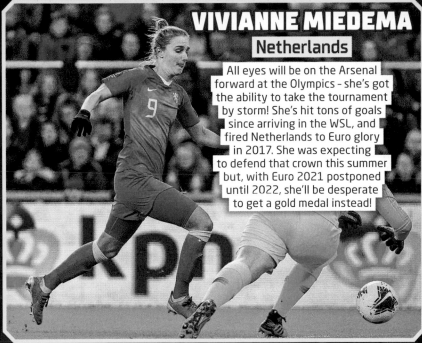

VIVIANNE MIEDEMA
Netherlands

All eyes will be on the Arsenal forward at the Olympics - she's got the ability to take the tournament by storm! She's hit tons of goals since arriving in the WSL, and fired Netherlands to Euro glory in 2017. She was expecting to defend that crown this summer but, with Euro 2021 postponed until 2022, she'll be desperate to get a gold medal instead!

FORMIGA
Brazil

Formiga could add to her phenomenal career if she makes it into Brazil's squad. She's the only player to have starred at every tournament since women's footy was introduced to the Olympics in 1996, and has more caps for her country than any other player! Can she end her career in the perfect way?

SAM KERR
Australia

Women's Super League fans have already had a glimpse of Kerr during her time at Chelsea, and she's proven why she's one of the best strikers in the world. She dragged The Matildas to the World Cup knockout round in 2019, and will need that form again in Tokyo. Australia goes mad for the Olympics, so if she can bring home a medal, she'll be a national hero!

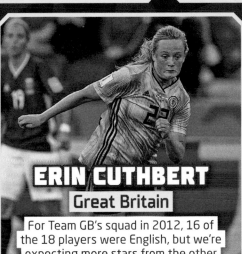

ERIN CUTHBERT
Great Britain

For Team GB's squad in 2012, 16 of the 18 players were English, but we're expecting more stars from the other home nations to be picked this time. Cuthbert will definitely be a contender - the Chelsea wonderkid already has loads of international caps, and was Scotland's best attacker at the World Cup. She'll add plenty of flair to the front line!

ROSE LAVELLE
USA

Legends like Rapinoe and Alex Morgan are in their 30s, so Lavelle is next in line to become the USA's next big star - and she could use the Olympics to prove it! She was named the third-best player at the 2019 World Cup, then finished sixth in the Ballon d'Or vote. With another two years' experience, the midfielder is ready to take over women's football!

STEPH HOUGHTON
Great Britain

Houghton will be one of the first names on the team sheet for Great Britain in Tokyo, and could wear the captain's armband too. The centre-back is a solid defender and inspirational leader, but she also finished as Team GB's top scorer at London 2012! As one of the few survivors from that squad, her experience will be vital in Japan!

KOSOVARE ASLLANI
Sweden

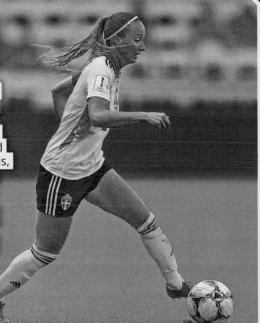

Asllani's form at the 2019 World Cup was enough to convince Real Madrid to make her one of their first female Galacticos! She fired her country to the semi-finals, three years after helping them win a silver medal in Rio, but this time she wants gold. With her flair and goalscoring ability, nobody will want to play against Sweden!

BIG MATCH! QUIZ

STRIKERS SPECIAL

You Tube STAR!

Which lethal goal machine has taken the place of Sammy from the Knuckleball Twins?

MATCH MATHS!

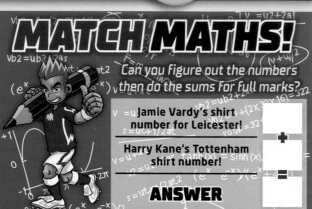

Can you figure out the numbers then do the sums for full marks?

Jamie Vardy's shirt number for Leicester!

Harry Kane's Tottenham shirt number!

+

=

ANSWER

FREAKY FACES!

Which sick Championship striker has been given a really wacky makeover in this crazy pic?

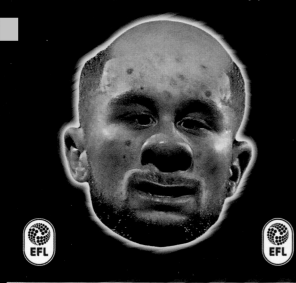

EFL   EFL

THE NICKNAME GAME!

MATCH these mega deadly strikers to their wicked nicknames!

Raul Jimenez	Marcus Rashford	Karim Benzema	Robert Lewandowski
1	**2**	**3**	**4**

A	**B**	**C**	**D**
Beans	The Cat	Pencil Sharpener	The Body

GROUNDED!

Name Belgium goal grabber Romelu Lukaku's amazing home ground!

FOOTY MIS-MATCH

Can you spot the ten differences between these pics of England hot-shot Ellen White?

1		6	
2		7	
3		8	
4		9	
5		10	

ANSWERS ON PAGE 94

STRIKERS WORDFIT!

Fit 30 lethal forwards into this monster grid!

Abraham	Immobile	Miedema
Aguero	Ings	Milik
Aspas	Jesus	Morgan
Beckie	Kane	Popp
Benzema	Kerr	Ronaldo
Bremer	Lacazette	Suarez
England	Le Sommer	Vela
Firmino	Marta	Werner
Hegerberg	Mbappe	White
Icardi	Messi	Zapata

R O N A L D O

ANSWERS ON PAGE 94

LEGENDS

2020

DE BRUYNE

ERLING HAALAND

THE WORLD'S BEST WONDERKID!

MATCH tells the story behind Haaland's rise to the top of European football!

LIKE FATHER, LIKE SON!

Erling was born in Leeds while his dad, Alf-Inge, was a Premier League player. Haaland senior was a tough-tackling defensive midfielder for Nottingham Forest, Leeds, Man. City and Norway, but his son has way more talent. He's been destined for great things from an early age, and made his senior debut for his first club Bryne – the same team his dad broke through at – when he was just 15!

BIG BREAKOUT!

After a year at Bryne, Erling joined Molde to link up with one of Norway's all-time greats. His new boss, Ole Gunnar Solskjaer, gave him tips on how to become a world-class striker and, within a couple of years, he was one of Norway's deadliest hitmen! In 2018, he was the third-highest scorer in the league with 12 goals, and bagged four goals in five Europa League games!

UNDER-20 SUPERSTAR!

By 2019, Haaland was beginning to build a reputation as one of the hottest young talents in Europe. A year on from scoring nine goals in just nine U19 Euro qualifying games for Norway, he made headlines at the U20 World Cup. The red-hot striker put in an absolutely devastating performance against Honduras, scoring an incredible TRIPLE hat-trick in an amazing 12-0 win!

SALZBURG STAR!

Haaland took that sizzling form into his first full season at RB Salzburg. In August 2019, he scored in every league match, bagging eight goals in five games, then another seven in his next six! He bossed the Champions League too, becoming the first player in history to score six goals in their first three games, and ended the group stage with eight net-busters!

WORLD'S MOST WANTED!

In total Erling spent less than 12 months in Austria, but he had an incredible impact – scoring 29 goals in 27 games! When the 2020 January transfer window opened, every club in Europe wanted him, including his old manager Solskjaer. The wonderkid visited Old Trafford, but chose to prove himself at Borussia Dortmund instead, and he's done exactly that - after hitting a hat-trick on his debut, he went on to bag 12 goals in his first eight games!

WHAT'S NEXT?

Haaland signed for Dortmund because he wanted to prove himself before joining one of Europe's mega giants, and he's definitely done that so far! His transfer value is sure to fly up over the next couple of years, and the race is already on to see who will get him - but first he wants to shine on the international stage for Norway at the Euros!

FACTPACK

Full name: Erling Braut Haaland

Age: 20 **Position:** Striker

Club: B. Dortmund **Country:** Norway

Boots: Nike Mercurial Vapor

Value: £105 million

TOP SKILLS

Finishing	10
Strength	9
Speed	8
Movement	8
Heading	8

TURN OVER FOR MATCH'S WONDERKID XI!

WONDER

ADIL AOUCHICHE

Aouchiche was a star for France Under-17s in 2019 - he fired them to the semi-finals at the Euros with nine goals in five games, then bagged seven assists and the Silver Ball at the World Cup a few months later! He made his Ligue 1 debut for PSG at the start of 2019-20, then became their second-youngest goalscorer in history in January 2020 before leaving to join Saint-Etienne on a free transfer last summer!

ANSU FATI

Fati made headlines all over the world when he burst onto the scene at the start of 2019-20! He broke tons of records with his first tastes of senior footy, quickly becoming Barcelona's youngest goalscorer of all time and the third youngest in La Liga history, then followed that up by becoming the youngest Champions League goalscorer ever too! With Lionel Messi alongside him, his potential is absolutely frightening!

JOSHUA ZIRKZEE

Just like Erling Haaland, Zirkzee made an incredible impact on his Bundesliga debut. The game was level at 1-1 when he came off the bench against Freiburg in injury time and, within two minutes, he'd sealed the win with his first touch! He was a super sub again v Wolfsburg in the very next game with another winning goal, and is already being lined up as Robert Lewandowski's long-term replacement at the club!

Vandevoordt
Genk

Dest
Ajax

Saliba
Arsenal

Fati
Barcelona

Aouchiche
Saint-Etienne

Zirkzee
Bayern

KID XI!

ALPHONSO DAVIES

Bayern signed Davies as an exciting pacy winger, but since arriving in Germany he's turned into a top-class left-back. He's a tough tackler and, because he's so quick, it's almost impossible for wingers to get the better of him! The Canada wonderkid still has all the attacking ability that attracted Munich in the first place, so he's wicked going forward as well – he picked up bags of assists in 2019-20!

Badiashile
Monaco

Davies
Bayern

Camavinga
Rennes

Martinelli
Arsenal

Greenwood
Man. United

EDUARDO CAMAVINGA

It takes a seriously special talent to make such a big impact at such a young age. Camavinga was the youngest player in Rennes' history when he made his debut in 2019 aged 16 but, within a few months, he'd become one of their main men! The teenager kicked off 2019-20 by dominating the midfield in a 2-1 victory over PSG and, after that, he barely missed a game in one of the club's best seasons in years!

THE SUBS' BENCH

GK
Gavin Bazunu
Man. City & Republic Of Ireland

LWB
Bukayo Saka
Arsenal & England

MF
Billy Gilmour
Chelsea & Scotland

MF
Ryan Gravenberch
Ajax & Netherlands

MF
Jude Bellingham
B. Dortmund & England

MF
Reinier
Real Madrid & Brazil

FW
Rodrygo
Real Madrid & Brazil

THE G.O.A.Ts

Bobby Moore
1958-1983

Country: England

Main Clubs: West Ham, Fulham

GOAT Credentials: The classic English CB is strong, brave and a beast in the air, but Moore was different. He didn't need to bully strikers, because he read what they were going to do and timed his tackles to perfection! He was just as classy with the ball, and set up England's fourth goal in the 1966 World Cup final, before minutes later lifting the trophy!

Franz Beckenbauer
1964-1983

Country: Germany

Main Clubs: Bayern Munich

GOAT Credentials: Franz Beckenbauer was the original sweeper – he was a master at mopping up attacks and getting his team up the pitch with an incisive pass or a driving run. He captained Germany to the 1974 World Cup, led Bayern to the European Cup three years in a row and is the only defender in history to win the Ballon d'Or twice!

CENTRE-BACKS

Now we move onto the best ever centre-backs – the defenders who bossed the opposition's strikers into submission!

Fabio Cannavaro
1992-2011

Country: Italy

Main Clubs: Parma, Juventus, Real Madrid

GOAT Credentials: Fabio Cannavaro played a key role in making Parma a Serie A force in in the 1990s, and helped Real Madrid win back-to-back La Ligas, but his greatest moment came at the 2006 World Cup. As Azzurri captain, he played every minute for the world champions, and went on to win the Ballon d'Or too!

Daniel Passarella
1971-1989

Country: Argentina

Main Clubs: River Plate, Fiorentina, Inter

GOAT Credentials: Daniel Passarella wasn't just a legendary defender and inspirational leader, he was also a prolific goalscorer. He hit 175 career goals for club and country, including 24 in one season for River Plate! He also led Argentina to World Cup glory on home soil in 1978 – the first WC trophy in the country's history!

HONOURABLE MENTIONS

Ronald Koeman

Alessandro Nesta

Rio Ferdinand

John Charles

Gaetano Scirea

John Terry

Carles Puyol

Franco Baresi
1977-1997

Country: Italy

Main Clubs: AC Milan

GOAT Credentials: Standing at just 5ft 9ins with a skinny build, Baresi didn't look like a typical centre-back, but opposition forwards couldn't take him lightly - his tackles were rock solid and he had the pace to keep up with anybody! His brain was even quicker, though. The AC Milan and Italy skipper read the game like a book, and was always in the right place to end attacks. That's why he was the best defender in the world, winning three European Cups and six Serie A titles. Legend!

PRETENDERS
These stars will enter the GOAT conversation when they eventually retire!

Sergio Ramos
Real Madrid & Spain

Ramos has a trophy haul to match any player in history, with La Ligas, Champions Leagues, Club World Cups, Euros and a World Cup in his cabinet. Wow!

Gerard Pique
Barcelona & Spain

Alongside Ramos, Barcelona legend Pique made Spain's defence absolutely world class, while winning tons of trophies for club and country too!

Virgil van Dijk
Liverpool & Netherlands

Van Dijk is the complete defender - he's impossible to dribble past and has made Liverpool's defence one of the best in the world over the past few years!

Mats Hummels
B. Dortmund & Germany

Hummels was a star of the Dortmund side that won back-to-back league titles under Jurgen Klopp, he won the World Cup with Germany, and then starred for Bayern!

Thiago Silva
PSG & Brazil

As well as being a total beast of a defender and at the top of his game for over a decade, Silva is a born leader - he's captained both club and country!

Raphael Varane
Real Madrid & France

In 2018, Varane became the ninth player in history to win the World Cup and the Champions League in the same year! Legendary status secured!

MATCH! CHATS TO THE STARS!

MATCH chatted to tons of football's biggest heroes in 2019-20! Get a load of the best quotes that featured in our weekly magazine over the past 12 months...

TYRONE MINGS

The Aston Villa and England defender's rise to the top has been incredible!

TYRONE SAYS: "When I was a mortgage advisor playing non-league footy, playing for England seemed a different world away! I've had to reassess my goals after some injuries, but that just makes it so much sweeter to now be a Premier League and England player!"

DELE ALLI

Dele told us all about why he loves his all-time footy hero – Steven Gerrard!

DELE SAYS: "Steven Gerrard is my hero because he's an England legend, and the mentality he had as Three Lions captain – I just loved watching him! I wouldn't say I based my game on him, but I really enjoyed watching him and his passion."

JORDAN PICKFORD

We asked the Everton and England goalkeeper about the best and worst dressers in The Toffees' changing room...

JORDAN SAYS: "Tom Davies has his own fashion sense - he wears some mad clothes... that's all I'll say! And just for the banter, I'll say Gylfi Sigurdsson has a dodgy fashion sense as well!"

VIRGIL VAN DIJK

It's no surprise Liverpool were so dominant in the Prem – according to VVD, their changing room mentality is ruthless!

VIRGIL SAYS: "Everybody was still enjoying winning the Champions League when we came back, but straight away it was down to playing again. We have to work hard in every match to stay focused on making a good start and push on!"

TAMMY ABRAHAM

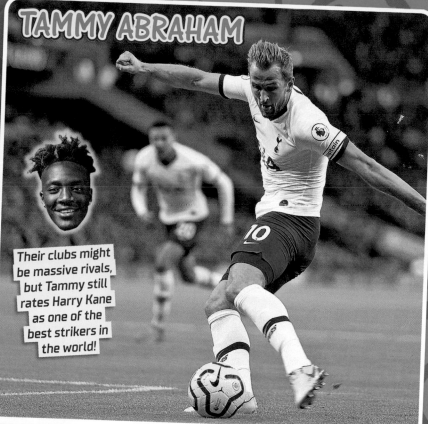

Their clubs might be massive rivals, but Tammy still rates Harry Kane as one of the best strikers in the world!

TAMMY SAYS: "I look at him and see a fantastic striker. When he gets the ball, everyone's off their seat! He's one of the best strikers in the world, and I want to be on that level! He's absolutely ruthless - every time he takes a shot, people think that he's going to score, and that's something I've got to get into my game!"

RAPHAEL VARANE

The world-class defender gave us an insight into what it takes to make it at Real Madrid!

RAPHAEL SAYS: "The pressure is as huge as it can get. That's why not all footballers can play at a club like Real Madrid - the club and fans demand that we always play to our best! You need to have the right mentality to be able to perform to your best week in, week out!"

DECLAN RICE

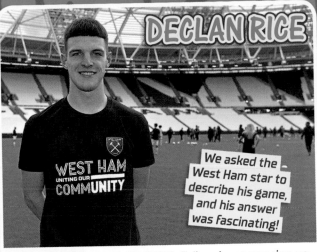

We asked the West Ham star to describe his game, and his answer was fascinating!

DECLAN SAYS: "When I was growing up as a defender, I had to be able to read the game. So, as I've stepped into midfield, I've taken that with me. Getting into positions where my defenders want me to be or to intercept a pass is one of my strengths!"

LUKE SHAW

Shaw gave MATCH the lowdown on Man. United's best youngsters, and he was full of praise for one star in particular...

LUKE SAYS: "Mason Greenwood is two-footed in a way I've not seen for ages. His skills and finishing are a joke, but both of his feet are perfect - he takes corners with his left and free-kicks with his right! He's an unbelievable striker!"

MASON MOUNT

Frank Lampard's had a huge influence on Mount's career, and the wonderkid told us all about his relationship with his boss!

MASON SAYS: "We talk every day on what I can do better - where I can make runs, where to get into the box and how to pick a corner rather than snatching at shots. As an attacking midfielder, I couldn't learn off anyone better!"

BIG MATCH! QUIZ

MIDFIELDERS SPECIAL

GAME CHANGER!

Name the Atletico ace who came on as a sub and scored twice at Anfield in 2019-20!

THE NUMBERS GAME!

How many Premier League matches did Kevin De Bruyne play for Chelsea in 2013?

TROPHY TIME!

Which WSL midfielder is hiding behind the trophy?

NAME THE NATION!

Name the countries that these midfield machines play for!

1. Julie Ertz

2. Amandine Henry

3. Dzsenifer Marozsan

4. Caroline Graham Hansen

5. Danielle van de Donk

6. Saki Kumagai

Youri Tielemans

Joao Moutinho

Abdoulaye Doucoure

Granit Xhaka

Giovani Lo Celso

N'Golo Kante

ODD ONE OUT!

Which of these awesome CMs has never played in France?

MEGA MASH-UP!

Name the pass master in this pic from 2019-20!

ACTION REPLAY

How much can you remember about Man. United's mega signing of huge fans' fave Bruno Fernandes?

1 True or False? United signed Fernandes on Deadline Day of the Summer 2019 window!

2 Name the Portuguese club that The Red Devils signed him from!

3 How much did he cost - more or less than £45 million?

4 True or False? Man. United will have to pay even more for him if they win the Prem title with Fernandes in their squad!

5 What shirt number was Bruno handed?

6 When did his initial contract run until - 2023, 2024 or 2025?

7 Who did he make his Prem debut against - Chelsea or Wolves?

8 And who did he score his first Prem goal against?

9 True or False? He won the Prem Player Of The Month prize in his first month in England!

ANSWERS ON PAGE 94

Midfielders BRAIN-BUSTER!

How well do you know these midfielders?

1. What is Toni Kroos' funny nickname – the waiter, the chef or the cleaner?

2. Which England midfielder is older – Jill Scott or Lucy Staniforth?

3. What club did Barcelona sign Frenkie de Jong from in the summer of 2019?

4. What home nation does Aston Villa midfielder John McGinn play for?

5. Which epic boot brand does Jorginho wear – Nike, adidas or Puma?

6. Which superstar midfielder has played more Prem matches for Liverpool – Fabinho or Georginio Wijnaldum?

7. True or False? Keira Walsh has spent her enitre pro career at Man. City!

8. What country did legendary Arsenal midfielder Patrick Vieira play for?

9. Which manager wasn't a midfielder – Pep Guardiola, Mauricio Pochettino, Frank Lampard or Zinedine Zidane?

10. Which country has Arsenal's Kim Little not played in – Australia, Scotland, United States or Spain?

1 ....
2 ....
3 ....
4 ....
5 ....
6 ....
7 ....
8 ....
9 ....
10 ....

ANSWERS ON PAGE 94

DRAW YOUR FAVE CARTOON!

If you love all the cool footy cartoons in MATCH, then you'll love this!
Check out some of our faves, and draw a cartoon of your own hero!

BUILD A DREAM TEAM!

MATCH wants to create a new team to take over English football, but we need your help to pick the players from this awesome shortlist! We've got a transfer budget of £500 million – can you build a team of world beaters?

Send us your XI for the chance to win a mind-blowing gaming bundle!

GOALKEEPERS

Who's gonna be between the sticks?

JAN OBLAK
ATLETICO MADRID

The multiple winner of La Liga's awesome Zamora Trophy – which is awarded to the keeper with the lowest goals-to-game ratio – is a superstar shot-stopper! MATCH fans on social media actually voted Oblak as the best goalie in the world in 2020!

£70M

ALISSON
LIVERPOOL

MATCH reckons Alisson is the most valuable GK on the planet – his arrival helped transform Liverpool into Prem and European champions! The Brazilian would be a proper expensive addition, but can you really put a price on consistent clean sheets?

£75M

MARC-ANDRE TER STEGEN
BARCELONA

If you want to build a team that's going to dominate possession, you'll need a goalkeeper who's comfortable with the ball at their feet – and Ter Stegen is the best around! He basically plays as an extra centre-back for Barcelona!

£60M

OR...

THIBAUT COURTOIS
REAL MADRID
£55 million

EDERSON
MAN. CITY
£50 million

BERND LENO
ARSENAL
£30 million

NICK POPE
BURNLEY
£15 million

JORDAN PICKFORD
EVERTON

The Everton No.1 is already an established Premier League and international goalkeeper, with one of the longest kicks MATCH has ever seen! His awesome agility, penalty stops and rapid reflexes make him a rock-solid choice!

£25M

DEAN HENDERSON
MAN. UNITED

If you want to invest in the future, but also save some bucks, we recommend turning to Hendo! He had a fantastic first season in the Prem on loan at Sheffield United, and proved that he's ready for your No.1 jersey!

£20M

£40M

GIANLUIGI DONNARUMMA
AC MILAN

In the Italian, you'll be signing a goalkeeper in their early twenties with over 200 senior club appearances already, plus double figures for international caps! You won't have to worry about replacing him for another decade!

CENTRE-BACKS

Choose from these top-quality defenders!

RAPHAEL VARANE
REAL MADRID

Frenchman Varane has already lifted the World Cup, Champions League, La Liga and Spanish Super Cup trophies, but what he really wants to get his hands on is the Premier League and FA Cup double for your dream team!

£70M

£75M

VIRGIL VAN DIJK
LIVERPOOL

Buying probably the best CB on the planet was never going to be cheap, but are you willing to spend close to a fifth of your entire budget on him? Don't worry, MATCH isn't going to judge you if you do!

TYRONE MINGS
ASTON VILLA

We reckon £30 million is a total bargain for an England defender who's in his prime years, but don't let us influence you! He's not the quickest, so it might be useful to pair him with someone pacy!

£30M

OR...

JOSE GIMENEZ
ATLETICO MADRID
£50 million

DAVINSON SANCHEZ
TOTTENHAM
£30 million

MICHAEL KEANE
EVERTON
£25 million

BEN GODFREY
NORWICH
£20 million

DAYOT UPAMECANO
RB LEIPZIG

The young centre-back joined RB Leipzig for less than £10 million in 2017, but his value has already quadrupled! He's one of the toughest defenders on the planet, great in possession and can out-jump most strikers in aerial battles!

£45M

GERARD PIQUE
BARCELONA

Bargain alert! The veteran CB probably only has a couple more top-quality campaigns left in him, but he could provide the experience and leadership your side needs to mount a title challenge – and then employ him as a coach!

£15M

£65M

MATTHIJS DE LIGT
JUVENTUS

It's so easy to forget that De Ligt only turned 21 years old last summer – he's already a star name in world football and playing regularly for one of the best defensive units on the planet. Invest in the Netherlands superstar for now and the future!

AYMERIC LAPORTE
MAN. CITY

Man. City's struggles while Laporte was out injured for long parts of the 2019-20 season showed what an important player he is for his side! He won 43 of his first 50 league matches for City – setting a new Premier League record!

£55M

£65M

HARRY MAGUIRE
MAN. UNITED

Not every player has the leadership traits and bottle to captain one of the biggest clubs on the planet – and it's even more impressive that Maguire was made Red Devils skipper in the same season he joined the club!

OR...

MILAN SKRINIAR
INTER
£50 million

WILLIAM SALIBA
ARSENAL
£35 million

JAMAAL LASCELLES
NEWCASTLE
£20 million

LEWIS DUNK
BRIGHTON
£20 million

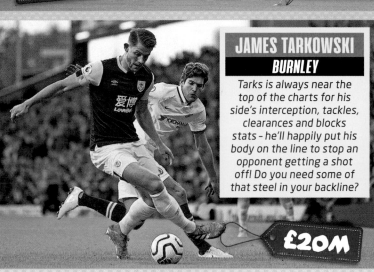

JAMES TARKOWSKI
BURNLEY

Tarks is always near the top of the charts for his side's interception, tackles, clearances and blocks stats – he'll happily put his body on the line to stop an opponent getting a shot off! Do you need some of that steel in your backline?

£20M

CAGLAR SOYUNCU
LEICESTER

Leicester fans love Soyuncu – he stepped up big time when Maguire left the club! As well as being a monster in the air and a top tackler, he's got silky technique on the ball, so he's perfect if you want to play out from defence!

£35M

£60M

£18M

FIKAYO TOMORI
CHELSEA

After some really tough negotiations with the Blues bosses, we've managed to get a proper discount on the England youngster! Snap him up for less than £20 million, and watch him grow into a £50 million star within a few solid seasons!

KALIDOU KOULIBALY
NAPOLI

Napoli fans affectionately know the rock-solid Senegal defender as 'The Wall', because he's so hard to dribble past! He's not just a tough tackler, though – he's comfortable carrying the ball forward into midfield and starting attacks!

FULL-BACKS

Pick a flying full-back for either flank!

GEORGE BALDOCK
SHEFFIELD UNITED

He might not be such an exciting name on paper as some of the other options on this shortlist, but in Baldock you'll have a rock-solid Premier League defender for a cut-price deal – meaning you can save important funds for other areas!

£15M

ACHRAF HAKIMI
INTER

As well as bagging double figures for assists in 2019-20, Hakimi, who can play at left or right-back, was also one of the Bundesliga's most successful dribblers on loan at Dortmund! That led to Inter going all out to sign him – will you do the same?

£55M

JORDI ALBA
BARCELONA

A few seasons ago, Alba would've been worth double – but now he's moving further into his 30s, you can sign him for a lot less! He's still got the pace and energy to race up and down the pitch like he's been doing for over a decade!

£40M

OR...

ANDY ROBERTSON
LIVERPOOL
£60 million

DAVID ALABA
BAYERN MUNICH
£45 million

BRANDON WILLIAMS
MAN. UNITED
£15 million

PATRICK VAN AANHOLT
CRYSTAL PALACE
£20 million

MAX AARONS
NORWICH

The Three Lions are blessed with tons of attacking full-backs, and Aarons was the latest to make a name for himself in 2019-20 for Norwich! As well as being absolutely rapid, he's also got the vision to find team-mates in good positions!

£25M

MARCELO
REAL MADRID

He might be nearing the end of his career, but shirt sales would go through the roof if you managed to sign the Brazilian trickster! He's still got the talent to get fans onto their feet with his silky skills and brilliant ball control!

£20M

£50M

BEN CHILWELL
LEICESTER

Chilwell's rise over the past two seasons has been absolutely astronomical! He's gone from being a breakthrough academy prospect to one of the best left-backs on the planet – and England's first choice! Reckon he's worth that hefty price tag, though?

ALPHONSO DAVIES
BAYERN MUNICH

Watching Davies stampede forward with the ball is one of the greatest sights in footy – there's no stopping him once he reaches full pelt! That's what you get when a winger converts to a full-back – pure attacking gold!

£45M

£28M

OR...

ALEX SANDRO
JUVENTUS
£40 million

KIERAN TIERNEY
ARSENAL
£30 million

RICARDO PEREIRA
LEICESTER
£35 million

LUCAS DIGNE
EVERTON
£30 million

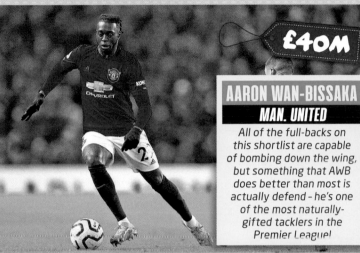

£40M

AARON WAN-BISSAKA
MAN. UNITED

All of the full-backs on this shortlist are capable of bombing down the wing, but something that AWB does better than most is actually defend – he's one of the most naturally-gifted tacklers in the Premier League!

REECE JAMES
CHELSEA

Another young prospect with huge potential is James! He's a quality all-round defender with a big footy brain – that's how he can operate smoothly on either flank, as a CB or even as a defensive midfielder!

MATT DOHERTY
WOLVES

The Republic Of Ireland international has made a name for himself as a Fantasy Football must – a defender who'll be sure to grab you points with his goals, assists and chances created! At £20 million, he's cheap as chips too!

£20M

£80M

BUKAYO SAKA
ARSENAL

Just like Alphonso Davies, Arsenal rising star Saka was re-trained as a full-back last season. He's more comfortable playing further forward and sees plenty of action for The Gunners as a wing-back, midfielder or winger, and that versatility is priceless!

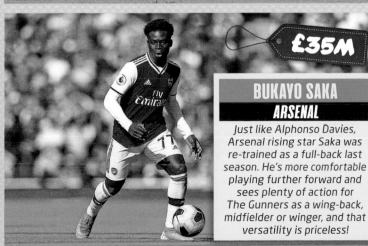

£35M

TRENT ALEXANDER-ARNOLD
LIVERPOOL

We reckon your heart sunk when you saw that price tag, but bear in mind that free-kick demon Trent was rated the best full-back in the world in the 2019 FIFA Ballon d'Or vote, so his guaranteed assists aren't going to come cheap!

MIDFIELDERS
Who's going to boss the middle of the park?

FRENKIE DE JONG
BARCELONA

De Jong has played for two of Europe's 'Total Football' sides – passing masters Ajax and Barca! He's able to collect the ball in midfield under pressure, shimmy away from his man and move the ball onto a team-mate. Class!

£55M

JOSHUA KIMMICH
BAYERN MUNICH

Any player that can perform just as well in two different positions deserves MATCH's respect – like Kimmich! He started off as a solid right-back, but has since moved into central midfield – and doesn't look out of place whatsoever!

£45M

£70M

KEVIN DE BRUYNE
MAN. CITY

If you're thinking about playing with a 4-2-3-1 formation, surely De Bruyne was in your mind as the CAM? He grabbed more assists than any other Premier League hero in 2019-20, and has almost-perfect passing precision!

OR...

GIOVANI LO CELSO
TOTTENHAM
£40 million

RUBEN NEVES
WOLVES
£40 million

THOMAS PARTEY
ATLETICO MADRID
£40 million

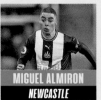

MIGUEL ALMIRON
NEWCASTLE
£25 million

SANDRO TONALI
BRESCIA

The wicked wonderkid has been one to watch since starring for Brescia at a young age, and he received huge praise from Italy legend Andrea Pirlo – he said Tonali was a more complete player than he was! We'll take that for £30 million!

£30M

WILFRED NDIDI
LEICESTER

Basically all of the best teams rely on a defensive midfielder to protect the defence, allowing the attack-minded stars to play with freedom! There aren't many betters DMs in the world right now than the Foxes and Nigeria warrior!

£30M

£65M

BRUNO FERNANDES
MAN. UNITED

It's a sign of Fernandes' ability that he was able to move to the Premier League halfway through a season and settle in straightaway! He won the club's Player Of The Month award in his first month and totally transformed The Red Devils' form!

PAUL POGBA
MAN. UNITED

Pog hasn't quite hit the heights expected of him at Man. United when he signed for a club-record £89 million, but he's still the closest thing to the complete midfielder on the planet – he can pass, dribble, assist and score!

£60M

£65M

SAUL NIGUEZ
ATLETICO MADRID

One of our fave things about Saul is that he combines all his incredible technical qualities with a real desire to put a shift in – he loves seeing his name at the top of the 'distance run' charts! Massive respect for that, Saul!

£50M

JAMES MADDISON
LEICESTER

If you're planning on landing Foxes hero Madders, make sure you stick him straight on set-piece duties – he's one of the best around at hitting a dead ball! His best position is as an attacking midfielder, so think about a 4-2-3-1 with him in it!

OR...

KAI HAVERTZ
BAYER LEVERKUSEN
£60 million

DANI OLMO
RB LEIPZIG
£35 million

JUDE BELLINGHAM
BORUSSIA DORTMUND
£30 million

JAMES WARD-PROWSE
SOUTHAMPTON
£15 million

DECLAN RICE
WEST HAM

Here's another defensive midfield option – with the added bonus of Rice also being able to play as a centre-back! That allows you to change formation to a back five midway through the game if you're trying to hold on to a slender lead!

£40M

MASON MOUNT
CHELSEA

The England midfielder is still a couple of seasons away from being the finished article, but land him while he's still under £40 million and you can help him develop into the Premier League's next Frank Lampard!

£35M

£30M

JORDAN HENDERSON
LIVERPOOL

Any of Liverpool's CMs would be deserving of a place in your team, but we're shouting out to Hendo for becoming the first Liverpool captain to lift a league title for 30 years in 2019-20! His leadership skills rock!

WINGERS

Now you need to pick your side's wing kings!

HEUNG-MIN SON
TOTTENHAM

Sonny is a real fans' favourite among Spurs supporters – he's always smiling off the pitch, and on it he's their most direct dribbler! He's a real goalscoring winger, as well – he can finish with either his left or right foot!

£40M

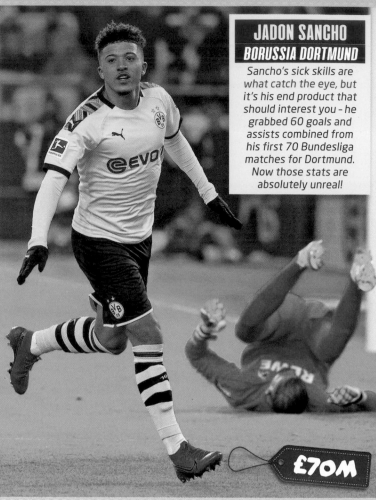

JADON SANCHO
BORUSSIA DORTMUND

Sancho's sick skills are what catch the eye, but it's his end product that should interest you – he grabbed 60 goals and assists combined from his first 70 Bundesliga matches for Dortmund. Now those stats are absolutely unreal!

£70M

ALLAN SAINT-MAXIMIN
NEWCASTLE

The fans on Tyneside have been treated to some total tricksters over the years – the likes of Peter Beardsley, David Ginola, Lomana LuaLua and Hatem Ben Arfa spring to mind! Now you can add Saint-Maximin to that list!

£30M

OR...

NEYMAR
PSG
£80 million

WILFRIED ZAHA
CRYSTAL PALACE
£40 million

LEROY SANE
BAYERN MUNICH
£50 million

EBERECHI EZE
QPR
£18 million

HARVEY BARNES
LEICESTER

Leicester supporters love Barnes for being 'one of their own' – he came through their youth academy, was sent out on loan and is now becoming a brilliant first-teamer under Brendan Rodgers. Is he going to be 'one of your own', too?

£25M

£60M

JARROD BOWEN
WEST HAM

Making the step up to the Premier League halfway through the 2019-20 season was never going to be easy for the ex-Hull wideman, but he's proven since that he's got the talent to tear up the top tier!

£20M

SADIO MANE
LIVERPOOL

Mane's most dangerous attribute is definitely his sizzling pace! Not only does he use it to speed past defenders, but he also terrifies full-backs by running full pelt at them when they receive the ball! Don't forget about his expert finishing skills either!

ADAMA TRAORE
WOLVES

As well as thinking about your favourite players, you need to bear in mind your tactics as well – do the players you're picking have the assets to play your fave style? Pick Adama if you want to attack with speed on the counter!

£40M

£45M

LIONEL MESSI
BARCELONA

If you've ever dreamt of having Messi in your side, now's the time to make it happen! The 33-year-old forward isn't too far away from retiring, but still has the ability to be a game changer with his incredible finishing and vision!

£50M

JACK GREALISH
ASTON VILLA

The great thing about Grealish is that he can play from a wide position or as an attacking central midfielder! He could be a good shout as part of an attacking three or four that plays with freedom and switches positions!

DWIGHT MCNEIL
BURNLEY

McNeil is one that got away for Man. United – The Red Devils rejected him when he was just 14 years old! The quick-footed winger has proven them wrong since then – he just needs to work on his consistency!

£25M

RAHEEM STERLING
MAN. CITY

The sizzling City star is right in the middle of his peak years, so you're going to have to part with a huge chunk of your budget to sign him! He started off as an exciting and speedy youngster, but has developed into a goal and assists machine!

£70M

£30M

DANIEL JAMES
MAN. UNITED

Ever since he scored that solo stunner for Swansea in the FA Cup in February 2019, James has been on MATCH's radar! He moved to United, had a sick first season and looks set for a long future at Old Trafford – unless you sign him!

STRIKERS

Which of these hitmen is gonna get your goals?

TIMO WERNER
CHELSEA

A 22-year-old Werner was thrown into the spotlight at the 2018 World Cup, but struggled as Germany were knocked out in the group stage! He's proven since then that he's no flop, top-scoring for Leipzig in every season before joining Chelsea!

£55M

RAUL JIMENEZ
WOLVES

Once upon a time, Jimenez was on loan at Spanish side Atletico Madrid – and he scored just one goal in 21 league matches! Fast forward five years and he's now one of the deadliest and most effective forwards in the Prem!

£40M

£75M

HARRY KANE
TOTTENHAM

If you end up signing the England captain, his club are going to make a huge profit – he came through Spurs' youth academy so he cost them nothing in transfer fees! You've just got to hope that he's over all his injuries!

OR...

LAUTARO MARTINEZ
INTER
£70 million

SERGIO AGUERO
MAN. CITY
£50 million

MASON GREENWOOD
MAN. UNITED
£30 million

ODSONNE EDOUARD
CELTIC
£25 million

ROBERT LEWANDOWSKI
BAYERN MUNICH

The only reason you can sign Lewandowski for such a decent price is because he's already in his 30s! He had his best season ever in 2019-20, scoring more than 40 goals in all competitions for the Bundesliga champions. Ledge!

£50M

JAMIE VARDY
LEICESTER

Vardy joined The Foxes over eight years ago, and has gone on to become a club legend! He fired them to the PL title in 2015-16, scoring in a record-breaking 11 games in a row, and has now joined the 100 Prem goal club!

£25M

£45M

CRISTIANO RONALDO
JUVENTUS

CR7 has already tallied up over £200 million in career transfer fees, and you can make that over £250 million if you add him to your team! He's worth £45 million in shirt sales alone – and he guarantees you leadership but, most importantly... GOALS!

MARCUS RASHFORD
MAN. UNITED

Man. United are one of the richest clubs in the world, so they've got no need to sell you one of their best players on the cheap – especially when he's a homegrown talent that absolutely loves the club!

£70M

£55M

PIERRE-EMERICK AUBAMEYANG
ARSENAL

Arsenal paid £56 million for Auba in 2018 and, although he's now two years older, his value hasn't gone down – he's still as lethal as ever! The Gabon Panther took less time than Thierry Henry to hit 50 Gunners goals!

OR...

ROMELU LUKAKU
INTER
£60 million

MAURO ICARDI
PSG
£55 million

CIRO IMMOBILE
LAZIO
£35 million

DANNY INGS
SOUTHAMPTON
£25 million

£45M

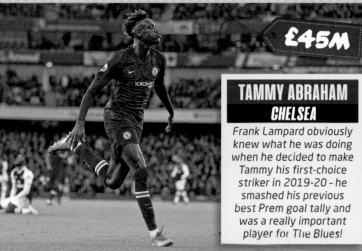

TAMMY ABRAHAM
CHELSEA

Frank Lampard obviously knew what he was doing when he decided to make Tammy his first-choice striker in 2019-20 – he smashed his previous best Prem goal tally and was a really important player for The Blues!

DOMINIC CALVERT-LEWIN
EVERTON

After scoring just 11 goals in his first 82 Prem games for Everton, Dom then scored 13 in his next 23 to establish himself as The Toffees' main goal grabber! Can you continue the good work Carlo Ancelotti has started?

£25M

£65M

£20M

JOSHUA ZIRKZEE
BAYERN MUNICH

If you can't afford Lewa, why not go for his long-term replacement at Bayern Munich – Netherlands wonderkid Zirkzee? The tall striker is a beast in the air, but he's also got great ball control and a surprising burst of pace!

ERLING HAALAND
BORUSSIA DORTMUND

Dortmund were able to steal Haaland for just £17 million in January 2019 thanks to his mega low release clause, but you guys aren't so lucky! His value has skyrocketed since taking the Bundesliga by storm with his wicked net-busters!

YOUR TEAM SHEET!

Fill in your team below, then take a picture and email it to MATCH! Don't forget, you've only got £500 million in total, so spend wisely and stick to your budget!

4-2-3-1

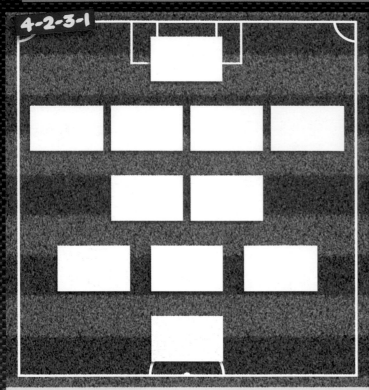

TOTAL COST:

4-3-3

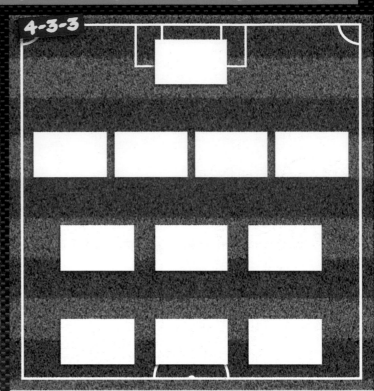

TOTAL COST:

4-4-2

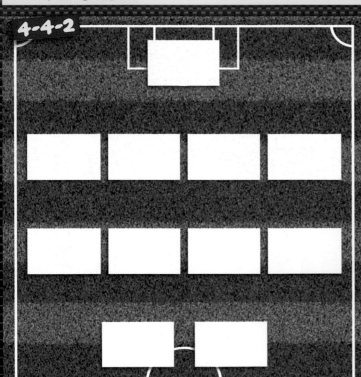

TOTAL COST:

 EMAIL YOUR TEAM SHEET TO:
match.magazine@kelsey.co.uk
Closing date: January 31, 2021.

LEGENDS

2020

INGS

FACTFILE!

Age: 28

Club: Southampton

Position: Striker

Value: £30 million

Country: England

Footy Fact! Ings busted 22 league nets last season for The Saints - his best-ever goal tally for a single season and Southampton's third-highest tally in a Prem campaign!

THE G.O.A.Ts

MATCH flicks through the football history books to take a closer look at the greatest players of all time!

Ashley Cole
1999-2019

Country: England

Main Clubs:
Arsenal, Chelsea

GOAT Credentials: Cristiano Ronaldo described Ashley Cole as his toughest ever opponent, and it's easy to see why - with his tenacity, defensive instincts and rapid pace, very few wingers got the better of the England man! He won 107 Three Lions caps and was one of Arsenal's Invincibles, before moving across London to win everything with Chelsea!

Carlos Alberto
1963-1982

Country: Brazil

Main Clubs:
Fluminense, Santos

GOAT Credentials: We've included three Brazilians in our top five - the country is the home of legendary attacking full-backs - and Alberto is one of their best! His greatest moment came in the 1970 World Cup final - he finished off a beautiful flowing move with a drilled finish to put the Samba Stars 4-1 up, before lifting the trophy as captain!

FULL-BACKS

These legends have all played their part in making the full-back role one of the most important positions in modern footy!

Cafu
1989-2008

Country: Brazil

Main Clubs: Sao Paulo, Roma, AC Milan

GOAT Credentials: By Brazil's next World Cup victory, they had another legendary right-back in the making. Cafu was a sub in the '94 final, but after that he hardly missed a minute. Like Alberto, he had tons of energy and quality to attack, plus the leadership ability to captain the team. He lifted the trophy as skipper in 2002, winning 142 caps!

Roberto Carlos
1991-2012

Country: Brazil

Main Clubs: Real Madrid

GOAT Credentials: While Cafu bossed Brazil's right flank, Carlos ran the left. With the demon duo, Brazil won two Copa Americas and reached two World Cup finals! The left-back loved to attack, and had a rocket left foot that made him deadly at free-kicks. After winning the World Cup and his third Champions League in 2002, he was pipped to the Ballon d'Or by team-mate Ronaldo!

HONOURABLE MENTIONS

 Djalma Santos

 Nilton Santos

Bixente Lizarazu

 Lilian Thuram

Gianluca Zambrotta

Javier Zanetti

 Philipp Lahm

PRETENDERS

These stars will enter the GOAT conversation when they eventually retire!

Dani Alves
Sao Paulo & Brazil

The most decorated player in history with over 40 trophies is still going strong back in his home country after a glittering career in Spain, Italy and France!

Marcelo
Real Madrid & Brazil

Brazil's incredible history of world-class full-backs is still alive today – Real Madrid legend Marcelo has been one of the best left-backs on the planet for ages!

Joshua Kimmich
Bayern Munich & Germany

Once Kimmich retires, he could end up being remembered as a legendary full-back or a top-class holding midfielder – he's simply world-class in both positions!

Jordi Alba
Barcelona & Spain

Alba's lightning-quick raids from left-back have been a big part of Barcelona and Spain's success over the last ten years! He's still got a few years left in him, though!

David Alaba
Bayern Munich & Austria

After making his name at left-back, Alaba switched to the centre of Bayern's defence in 2020! But, because he's so good, he also bosses the midfield for Austria!

Trent Alexander-Arnold
Liverpool & England

The youngster is already well on his way to becoming a Liverpool legend – he's one of the youngest Champions League winners in football history!

Paolo Maldini
1984-2009

Country: Italy

Main Clubs: AC Milan

GOAT Credentials: While most of the other full-backs in this top five were known for their amazing attacking ability, Maldini was a pure defender. At his peak, he was both the best centre-back and best left-back on the planet! He became Milan's youngest ever player when he made his debut aged 16, captained the side for more than half his career and made their defence the toughest in Europe. In total he played in eight European Cup finals across three decades, winning five, and played a record 902 games for Milan!

SNAPPED!
BEST OF 2020!

Marvel Magpie!

Allan Saint-Maximin learned a sick new skill in 2020!

I BELIEVE I CAN FLY!

Hair header!

When you mistime your jump, but have a ponytail to fall back on!

QUALITY CONNECTION!

Man bun fail!

GIVE ME TIME, MATCH!

Cristiano's attempt at a man bun was a total flop!

WELCOME TO CARLO'S CHANNEL!

Cool Carlo!

Ancelotti is always updating his TikTok!

Wet floor alert!

These guys must have missed the sign!

WHOOPS!

OUCH! THAT HURT!

Training trouble!

Don't get nutmegged in RB Leipzig training!

Spurs stinker!

Dele Alli just had to let one rip!

Copy cats!

Etienne Capoue and Glenn Murray kept copying each other!

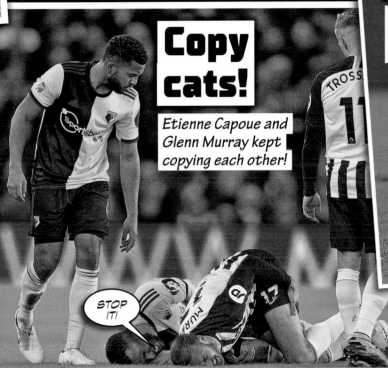

Yoga lesson!

Have you tried doing the 'Gareth Bale' stretch yet?

Weird wig!

This pic made it look like Andres Iniesta had hair extensions!

Nightmare Neymar!

That friend who always wants to try your food...

BIG MATCH! QUIZ

DEFENDERS SPECIAL

FLASHBACK!

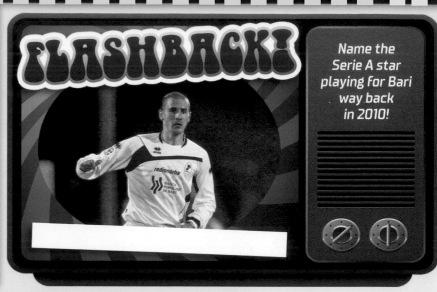

Name the Serie A star playing for Bari way back in 2010!

5 QUESTIONS ON...

STEPH HOUGHTON

1 Which Tyne-Wear derby rival did she start her career at – Sunderland or Newcastle?

2 How many Women's Super League titles did she win at Arsenal – two or three?

3 What year did Houghton join Man. City from The Gunners – 2013, 2014, 2015 or 2016?

4 Name the international trophy Steph captained England to victory in 2019!

5 True or False? She's won over 100 international caps for The Lionesses!

CLOSE-UP!

Which quality defenders have we zoomed in on?

1.

2.

3.

4.

CAMERA SHY!

Name the La Liga defenders hiding from the MATCH snapper in these pics!

Match these flying full-backs to their home stadiums!

Reece James	Patrick van Aanholt	Ben Chilwell	George Baldock
1	2	3	4
A	B	C	D
Selhurst Park	KP Stadium	Stamford Bridge	Bramall Lane

Name the Bundesliga CB in this weird pic!

BVB 09   BVB 09

Wolves

Newcastle

SUPER SKIPPERS!

Can you name these Prem teams' club captains?

Burnley

Man. United

WSL Heroes!

What teams do these WSL defenders play for?

1. Millie Bright

2. Gemma Bonner

3. Leah Williamson

4. Kristine Bjordal Leine

5. Jenna Schillaci

6. Gabby George

7. Gilly Flaherty

8. Amy Turner

CRAZY KIT!

Name the Chelsea CB in this bright kit from 2007-08!

ANSWERS ON PAGE 94

MEGA WORDSEARCH

Can you find these Flying full-backs in the mammoth grid?

```
L Y G K J D R                                               S X X K P U S
T G E A Y Q U                                               M I Z E F O S
H F W A J H D                                               Q U J T R Y Y
Y O X J A Z N                                               L S M Y D I L
G E V N I S E M E D O Y U A G Y N S I A D E O W G S Q O O D W
H F U G G W F Q B H O T Z O R R V W S Q T R I P P I E R T H X A
I M T P R D A V I E S A A E S B I W C F T U G D L D P J P E V N
L P E V E K P C Y R A S D N B W M M W Q K E J U O V I A Z R Y B
H Z G U E W L N F U T N A H W W A Z A Z R E L R L F G C O T H I
D I D T N V O I K M I I D W P K M L V L E X A L L E C M G Y A S
A M G V W I V E B L X J V E F M V E K L D W V T E E A P I O Z S
C I W X O H E C V X R C S P R E H P X E P O H D A S R A J J M A
X P K E O B X R W K Y K A G L S Z H E F R Q C Q V Y P I O N T K
A V E J D X D U Y O B O D H Q S N D B G N F G G C E I Y H B A
H Z C F C X V K G J L Z F N I A G O M R R K L V O B N C M Y D B
M Q K R P Y T A J A T F P S F I K Y N B R O N Z E Z T H E Z P Q
V D S F W A W B G R Q C G P O V Q I B Z X O M H M X E Z N Y J A
K J X D C C N S L F V G S E A N B N M U R U H U N O R V D O H A
S M R Q A F B A C A H J S R P Y H G W I K C T K D W K H Y Q I R
B G K Y R K X N H X C R H E P A C U N G J S D L U G H K S G T O
K A Y N V L T D I X T J R I S T O K E S N O O J N A E W L L D N
K N T Q A Y Y R L V W R K R M C M O I V L R R U N L R X P A Z S
M E Z L J Q Z O W B B L C A S G W X L J I M N X Z K N V B S S S
F J N Q A E F F E Y V V Y I T Z H I F Z E D C D I T H A V B C Y S
X N B T L A E F L R I T I E R N E Y R C T R A P V P N T D M M H
H T R E Z Y G K L T D H S Y K C A R D C R U K H D B D P U A M O
O G Q G C F E B F Y X K C C B D E Y W F S O U Q G J E X I M G L
O I E M G A V P J M N S M R W U A P W V C A L S E B Z L F P R E
T G A Z K E S G S K F U P X G V Q K Q I I K M M S L E W A I B
Z E T A H J E T Y F N T W P H V D F F V N N H L E I F X O V V A
I V A T F J A X A O U P B Y M S O A M K H S R T W A S E W A M S
T K L Z Q N W T S A E M B T D U I N Q O L A W N X M H Y H R B G
D D Q O R D M T B I U J T L R L E T V N V U V E C W C J W D N I
R D B E L H R A O O B E Z T G D J K R N K F Q W F U B C P K T J
C I B L Z E L F Q Q G T E A L A L E X A N D E R A R N O L D E P
E V C K B A Y R X R J A T E Z P G P K M V L M Z T H V M I U A T S
Q N A O R F J L A X V B J A K B E L L E R I N F Q Q F W C L M S
K V R R U U F T S V L M O K Q Y X L E M X N V R Z S M R N K U T
Q W E J D J V F J S X V X E Y B O G L H F Q A D T I B I J C X S T P
```

Aarons	Atal	Carvajal	Dunn	Hakimi	Mjelde	Semedo	Tierney
Alaba	Bellerin	Chilwell	Glas	Hernandez	Pavard	Stokes	Trippier
Alba	Bernat	Davies	Greenwood	Holebas	Pereira	Tagliafico	Walker
Alexander-Arnold	Bronze	Digne	Grimaldo	Mendy	Robertson	Targett	Wan-Bissaka
Andersson	Carpenter	Doherty	Guerreiro	Meunier	Sandro	Telles	Williams

ANSWERS ON PAGE 94

LEGENDS

2020

WAN-BISSAKA

MANCHESTER UNITED

FACTFILE!

Age: 22

Club: Man. United

Position: Right-back

Value: £60 million

Country: England

Footy Fact! When Aaron joined United for £50 million in 2019, he became the most expensive uncapped English footballer of all time - double the value of the next player on the list!

STARS' CARS!

Football's biggest superstars love splashing monster cash on flashy wheels! Here's some of the best...

MANE

THIS CAR WOULD DO WELL IN FORMULA 1 RACING!

ROLLS ROYCE PHANTOM

Price: £360,000
0–60: 5.8 seconds
Top Speed: 155mph

FIRMINO

BOBBY'S ALSO GOT A PORSCHE AND A 4X4. SICK!

BENTLEY BENTAYGA

Price: £162,700
0–60: 4 seconds
Top Speed: 187mph

MAHREZ

THIS CAR IS ALMOST AS FLASH AS FELIPE'S TEKKERS!

FERRARI F12 BERLINETTA

Price: £293,317
0–60: 3.1 seconds
Top Speed: 211mph

ANDERSON

PEPE

LAMBORGHINI AVENTADOR

Price: £271,146
0-60: 2.9 seconds
Top Speed: 217mph

POGBA

MCLAREN P1

Price: £866,000
0-60: 2.8 seconds
Top Speed: 217mph

INGS

MERCEDES SLS AMG

Price: £165,030
0-60: 3.8 seconds
Top Speed: 196mph

DG17 VHJ

FERRARI PORTOFINO

Price: £164,226
0-60: 3.5 seconds
Top Speed: 199mph

KEPA

FERRARI 812 SUPERFAST

LOVREN

Price: £253,000
0-60: 2.9 seconds
Top Speed: 211mph

THIS WAS DEJAN'S 30TH BIRTHDAY PRESENT FOR HIMSELF!

OBVIOUSLY THE MAN. CITY DEFENDER'S CAR IS BLUE. HERO!

RANGE ROVER OVERFINCH

Price: £205,000
0-60: 5.1 seconds
Top Speed: 140mph

LAPORTE

SAKHO

ROLLS ROYCE WRAITH

Price: £250,000
0-60: 4.1 seconds
Top Speed: 155mph

FERRARI LAFERRARI

SON

Price: £1,150,000
0-60: 2.4 seconds
Top Speed: 217mph

THE PREM'S MOST EXPENSIVE CAR IS OWNED BY SON AND AUBA!

LAMBORGHINI URUS

Price: £159,925

0-60: 3.6 seconds

Top Speed: 190mph

HALLER

THE BIG WEST HAM STRIKER NEEDS A BEASTLY CAR TO FIT IN!

FERRARI 458 ITALIA

Price: £178,390

0-60: 3 seconds

Top Speed: 211mph

PALACE ACE MAMADOU'S GOT TWO ROLLS ROYCES AND A BENTLEY!

JACK'S WHIP IS IN DARK CHROME RATHER THAN RED!

WILSHERE

BENTLEY GTC

Price: £163,700

0-60: 5.1 seconds

Top Speed: 195mph

CLEVERLEY

TOM WAS PROPER 'CLEVER' GETTING THIS MOTOR!

100 LG

THE G.O.A.Ts

MATCH flicks through the football history books to take a closer look at the greatest players of all time!

Zico
1971-1994
Country: Brazil

Main Clubs: Flamengo

GOAT Credentials: Brazil's 1982 side is regarded as the best World Cup team to never win the trophy. With players like Socrates, Falcao and Eder, the Samba Stars dazzled with their attacking style, but Zico was the star – he scored or assisted more than half of the team's goals! Although he missed out on the top prize, he did fire his club Flamengo to loads of silverware during his career!

Bobby Charlton
1956-1976
Country: England

Main Clubs: Man. United

GOAT Credentials: Before Wayne Rooney, Charlton was England and United's record scorer. The reason he got so many goals from midfield was simple – he had an absolute rocket of a shot that he could unleash with either foot from anywhere! He won the Ballon d'Or in the same year that England won the World Cup, and scored twice in the 1968 European Cup final!

MIDFIELDERS

Next we check out the greatest central midfield playmakers that could totally dominate games for their teams!

Michel Platini
1972-1987
Country: France

Main Clubs: Nancy, Saint-Etienne, Juventus

GOAT Credentials: Only Cristiano Ronaldo's scored as many goals at the Euros as Platini. But while CR7 has taken four tournaments and 21 games to hit nine goals, Platini did it one summer! In 1984 the midfielder was in the middle of winning three Ballons d'Or in a row, and dragged France to their first ever trophy by scoring in every single match. Wow!

Xavi
1998-2019
Country: Spain

Main Clubs: Barcelona

GOAT Credentials: From 2008 to 2012, Xavi was the king of European footy. During that time, Spain and Barcelona won everything and the midfield playmaker wasn't just a key player – he made everything tick! He hardly ever gave the ball away and always picked the right pass – whether he was helping his side dominate possession or unlocking the opposition's defence!

HONOURABLE MENTIONS

Lothar Matthaus

Ruud Gullit

Socrates

Claude Makelele

Kaka

Andrea Pirlo

Patrick Vieira

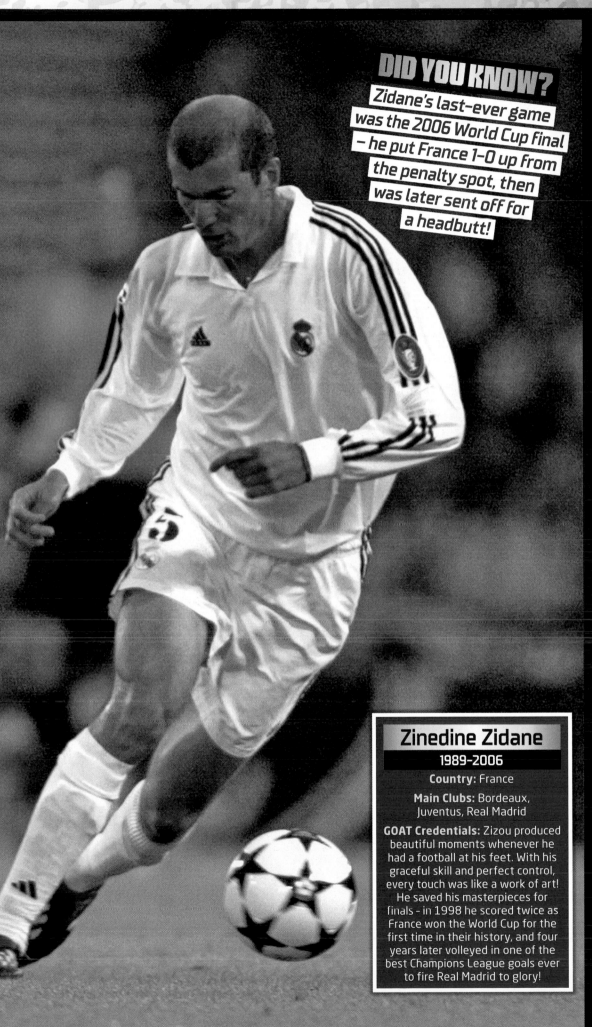

Zinedine Zidane

1989-2006

Country: France

Main Clubs: Bordeaux, Juventus, Real Madrid

GOAT Credentials: Zizou produced beautiful moments whenever he had a football at his feet. With his graceful skill and perfect control, every touch was like a work of art! He saved his masterpieces for finals - in 1998 he scored twice as France won the World Cup for the first time in their history, and four years later volleyed in one of the best Champions League goals ever to fire Real Madrid to glory!

PRETENDERS

These stars will enter the GOAT conversation when they eventually retire!

Andres Iniesta

Vissel Kobe & Spain

Alongside Xavi, midfield general Iniesta helped Spain and Barca dominate world football before heading over to Japan to see out his jaw-dropping career!

Sergio Busquets

Barcelona & Spain

The third and just as vital part of Barcelona and Spain's legendary midfield, Busquets is still going strong as one of the best DMs in the world!

Luka Modric

Real Madrid & Croatia

Modric played a crucial role in Real Madrid's four Champions League wins between 2014 and 2018, then led Croatia to the World Cup final in 2018!

Thomas Muller

Bayern Munich & Germany

Muller's World Cup record will put him in the history books! The lethal attacking midfielder/forward has hit ten goals - joint eighth on the all-time list!

Kevin De Bruyne

Man. City & Belgium

KDB has been one of the main reasons why Man. City have been so good over the last few years. He's simply unplayable - his footy brain, vision, passing and assists rock!

N'Golo Kante

Chelsea & France

One of the best DMs ever, Kante was playing in the French second division as recently as 2014, but since then has won two Prem titles and the World Cup!

F2

BECOMING YOUTUBE LEGENDS!

MATCH looks back at our best interviews with legendary footy freestylers THE F2 on how they become YouTube sensations!

FIRST PERFORMANCE!

BILLY SAYS: "I launched a shop on Bond Street in London for O2. I had to do tricks in the shop window – that was the very first job I did!"

JEZ SAYS: "Mine was for the opening of a gym, with TV presenter Bradley Walsh!"

BILLY SAYS: "Wait, I was there – that was my first job too! Wow, our first performances were technically with each other! I can't believe that... it was a terrible gym!"

LEARN FROM THE BEST!

JEZ SAYS: "Don't just think that those hours practising are all you need to improve your game. For example, if you're a left-back and want to improve that position, you could spend an hour and a half studying the best left-back in the world on a player cam, or turn the volume off on the TV and watch the game from a different perspective than a fan would. It's easy just to watch football as a fan, but trying to analyse a player can really help your game!"

CATCHPHRASES!

JEZ SAYS: "Sometimes we're on a pitch, and we'll just come up with something. One we thought of for killing the ball was 'deadsies', which obviously means stopping the ball dead! We just come up with them and they seem to catch on – we should try to create our own little tekkers dictionary!"

FOCUS ON FREESTYLE!

BILLY SAYS: "It was the biggest decision of my life to date. To give up football at 19 years old, when I was playing top-level semi-pro, one or two leagues away from being a professional. I saw an opportunity with the tricks... I was much closer to being the best at freestyling in the world than I was at playing. Why not try being the best in the world at something?"

WORKING WITH THE STARS!

JEZ SAYS: "We don't really get nervous around the players. Technically we're on the level of the pros, and we're confident in every situation in front of anyone. We get respect off the players, which is really good. We treat them as normal human beings, and have banter with them and crack jokes. They appreciate how relaxed we are."

BILLY SAYS: "I think they feel safe in our company. They've seen enough clips of our other videos with players and know we're not there to outdo them or make them look silly. When we meet players like Messi and Suarez, they're so open to us, which is a really good position to be in!"

TRAVELLING THE WORLD!

BILLY SAYS: "We did a Finding Football series, which saw us going to different countries and discovering football cultures and how they're different - what makes them work and what makes them unique! In Marseille everyone's playing footy everywhere, but the Brazilians, wherever you go, whoever they are, they love football! Iceland also took my breath away because it's such an extreme country, but Brazil was probably my favourite!"

MEETING NEYMAR!

BILLY SAYS: "We get to shoots four hours early to make sure everything's ready. There was a ball just sitting there waiting as Neymar walked onto the pitch for a PES shoot. He did what Neymar does, and pinged the ball into the top bins, first try! He just loves the ball, he loves the game! He took a picture with us and put it on his Instagram account saying, 'The phenomenons of freestyle'. That's just incredible!"

HOW MUCH PRACTICE?

BILLY SAYS: "It's hard to say in hours, but what I will say is this - if you want to be the best at something, you have to practise as much as you possibly can. That doesn't mean not doing your homework or helping out around the house - after doing all of those things, use your spare time to practise to give yourself the best chance to succeed. If you've done all of that and still don't succeed, then at least you can say you have given it everything!"

BIG MATCH! QUIZ

WONDERKIDS SPECIAL

FOOTY AT THE FILMS!

Which WSL ace is making a shock appearance in Wonder Woman 1984?

SPOT THE BALL!

Mark where you think the ball is in this cool action pic!

A B C D E F G H I

1 2 3 4 5 6 7 8 9 10 11 12 13 14 15 16 17 18 19

2019

2018

GUESS THE WINNERS!

Who won the Golden Boy award in these years?

2017

2016

FACE IN THE CROWD

Can you spot the ten highly-rated wonderkids below hiding somewhere within the footy crowd above?

Jadon Sancho

Ansu Fati

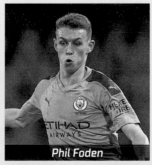

Phil Foden

Nicolo Zaniolo

Reece James

Gianluigi Donnarumma

Kai Havertz

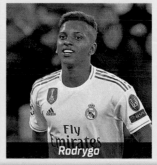

Max Aarons

Rodrygo

Sandro Tonali

ANSWERS ON PAGE 94

CROSSWORD CRUNCH!

Use these tricky clues to fill in MATCH's wonderkids crossword!

ACROSS

1. Position that PSG and Canada young gun Jordyn Huitema plays! (7)

4. Age that Mason Greenwood joined Man. United's awesome academy as a kid! (3)

6. Country that Jadon Sancho scored his first England goals against in September 2019! (6)

8. French team that Arsenal signed William Saliba from! (5,7)

11. First name of Reece James' wonderkid sister! (6)

15. Shirt number that Bukayo Saka wore in his first season for Arsenal's first team! (7,5)

17. Foot that Jude Bellingham prefers to use! (5)

18. Italian team that Barcelona's Ansu Fati hit his first Champions League goal against! (5,5)

19. Scottish city that Billy Gilmour grew up in as a child! (7)

20. German side that Bayern signed striker Fiete Arp from! (7)

DOWN

2. National team that Troy Parrott plays for! (8,2,7)

3. WSL side that forward Ebony Salmon tears it up for! (7,4)

5. Premier League team that Bayern Munich hero Alphonso Davies' dad supports! (7)

7. Month PSG megastar Kylian Mbappe was born! (8)

9. Shirt number that Georgia Stanway wears for Man. City! (3)

10. El Clasico side that Claudia Pina plays for! (9)

12. Club that Liverpool signed Harvey Elliott from! (6)

13. Portuguese side Florentino Luis made his debut for! (7)

14. Country that midfielder Lena Oberdorf represents! (7)

16. Boot brand that Wolves' Ruben Vinagre wears! (4)

ANSWERS ON PAGE 94

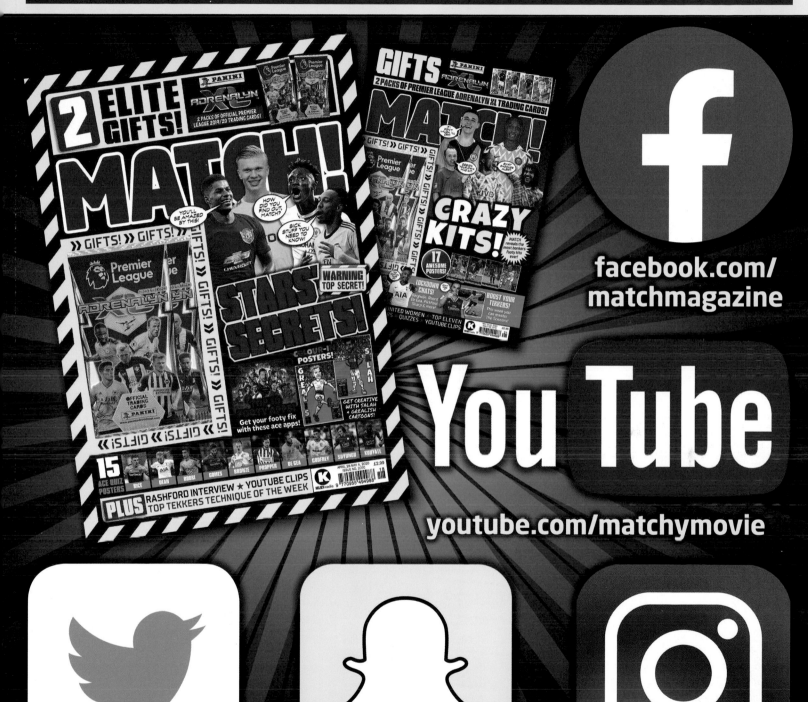

THE MOST SUCCESSFUL CLUBS...
IN THE WORLD!

MATCH goes globetrotting to find the clubs who've won the most trophies in world footy!

30		**AC MILAN** *Italy*	**48** TROPHIES
29		**RIVER PLATE** *Argentina*	**49** TROPHIES
28		**GRASSHOPPER** *Switzerland*	**49** TROPHIES
27		**DEPORTIVO SAPRISSA** *Costa Rica*	**53** TROPHIES
26		**CLUB OLIMPIA** *Paraguay*	**53** TROPHIES
25		**COLO-COLO** *Chile*	**53** TROPHIES
24		**CSKA SOFIA** *Bulgaria*	**55** TROPHIES
23		**BOCA JUNIORS** *Argentina*	**55** TROPHIES
22		**GALATASARAY** *Turkey*	**59** TROPHIES
21		**RED STAR BELGRADE** *Serbia*	**60** TROPHIES
20		**FCSB** *Romania*	**60** TROPHIES
19		**DYNAMO KIEV** *Ukraine*	**63** TROPHIES
18		**LIVERPOOL** *England*	**63** TROPHIES
17		**ANDERLECHT** *Belgium*	**64** TROPHIES
16		**MAN. UNITED** *England*	**66** TROPHIES

27 S

3 CN.of

5

26 OLIMPIA

25 COLO-COLO

29 CR

23 CABJ

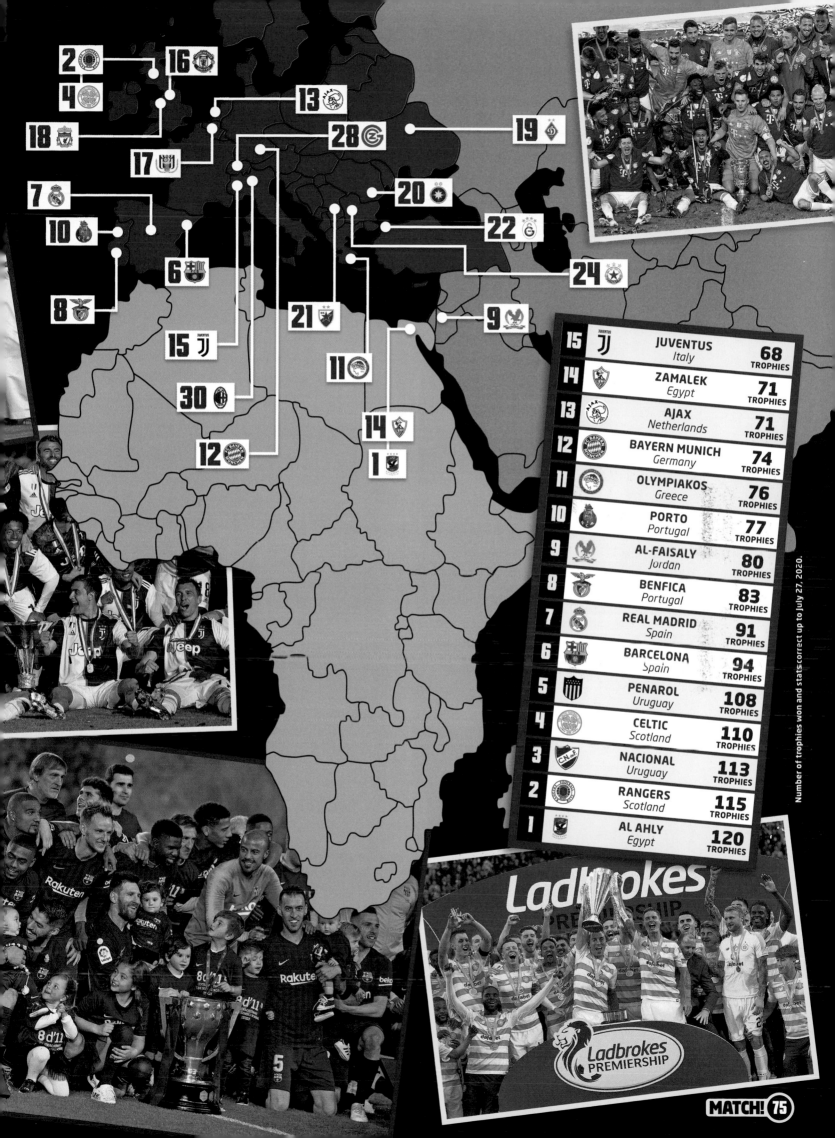

2 CELTIC

16 MANCHESTER UNITED

4 CELTIC

18 LIVERPOOL

13 AJAX

28 GRASSHOPPER

19 DYNAMO

17 ANDERLECHT

7 REAL MADRID

20

10 PORTO

22 GALATASARAY

6 BARCELONA

24

8 BENFICA

21 RED STAR

15 JUVENTUS

9 AL-FAISALY

30 AC MILAN

11 OLYMPIAKOS

12 BAYERN MUNICH

14 ZAMALEK

1 AL AHLY

15		JUVENTUS *Italy*	68 TROPHIES
14		ZAMALEK *Egypt*	71 TROPHIES
13		AJAX *Netherlands*	71 TROPHIES
12		BAYERN MUNICH *Germany*	74 TROPHIES
11		OLYMPIAKOS *Greece*	76 TROPHIES
10		PORTO *Portugal*	77 TROPHIES
9		AL-FAISALY *Jordan*	80 TROPHIES
8		BENFICA *Portugal*	83 TROPHIES
7		REAL MADRID *Spain*	91 TROPHIES
6		BARCELONA *Spain*	94 TROPHIES
5		PENAROL *Uruguay*	108 TROPHIES
4		CELTIC *Scotland*	110 TROPHIES
3		NACIONAL *Uruguay*	113 TROPHIES
2		RANGERS *Scotland*	115 TROPHIES
1		AL AHLY *Egypt*	120 TROPHIES

Number of trophies won and stats correct up to July 27, 2020.

THE G.O.A.Ts

MATCH flicks through the football history books to take a closer look at the greatest players of all time!

Stanley Matthews
1932-1965

Country: England

Main Clubs: Stoke, Blackpool

GOAT Credentials: It takes a special talent to have an FA Cup final named after them! In 1953, Blackpool were 3-1 down until 'The Wizard Of The Dribble' tore Bolton's defence apart, setting up three goals to bag the trophy! He regularly left a trail of defenders on the floor, and that's why he won the first-ever Ballon d'Or in 1956!

Ronaldinho
1998-2015

Country: Brazil

Main Clubs: Gremio, PSG, Barcelona, AC Milan

GOAT Credentials: Brazil legend Ronaldinho played with a smile on his face and magic in his boots, and was capable of doing things other players could only dream of! Within three years of joining Barca, they went from one of their worst-ever league positions to back-to-back La Liga titles and a Champions League, with star man Ron bagging the Ballon d'Or!

WINGERS

Now we get to wingers – the masters of tricky dribbling and outrageous skills that skinned defenders and created goals for their teams!

Garrincha
1951-1972

Country: Brazil

Main Clubs: Botafogo

GOAT Credentials: Fellow Brazilian Ronaldinho followed a long line of demon dribblers that began with Garrincha. At times, the right winger seemed more interested in embarrassing his opponents than winning matches, but that didn't stop him from firing Brazil to consecutive World Cups and finishing as top scorer in 1962! When he played alongside Pele, the Samba Stars never lost!

George Best
1963-1984

Country: Northern Ireland

Main Clubs: Man. United

GOAT Credentials: United's No.7 shirt is legendary and has been worn by some incredible players, but Best was the original. His dribbling ability was so good, he'd often beat a defender and wait for him to recover, then beat him again! He delivered in the biggest games too, scoring in the 1968 European Cup final as United won the trophy for the first time!

HONOURABLE MENTIONS

Paco Gento

Rivelino

Luis Figo

Ryan Giggs

Jairzinho

Robert Pires

David Beckham

Johan Cruyff
1964–1984
Country: Netherlands

Main Clubs: Ajax, Barcelona

GOAT Credentials: Nobody's had more of an influence on football in the last 50 years than Cruyff. Every team that he played for was known for playing slick, attacking, total football, and he wasn't just the star player either - he totally dominated matches! He could play in any position, and often spent games roaming all over the pitch to wherever the team needed him. He led Ajax to three European Cups in a row, before joining Barcelona for a world-record fee. Legend!

PRETENDERS
These stars will enter the GOAT conversation when they eventually retire!

Lionel Messi
Barcelona & Argentina

Many people think Messi is already the greatest footballer of all time! He could settle the argument if he finally guides Argentina to some silverware!

Cristiano Ronaldo
Juventus & Portugal

Like Leo, Ronaldo already belongs in a conversation about the greatest players in history. He's an incredible athlete too, so his career is far from over!

Neymar
PSG & Brazil

In terms of natural talent and pure skill, Neymar is as good as anybody in the world, but he's never won the Ballon d'Or award that his top footy tekkers deserve!

Eden Hazard
Real Madrid & Belgium

Hazard has already cemented his status as a Premier League great, but he'll have to prove himself as a world-beating Galactico to become an all-time legend!

Mohamed Salah
Liverpool & Egypt

Since he joined Liverpool, only Leo Messi has more goals in Europe's top five leagues than the Egyptian King - The Reds superstar just can't stop scoring!

Arjen Robben
Groningen & Netherlands

Wing wizard Robben was originally in our 'Honourable Mentions' before coming out of retirement in 2020! He just edges out Gareth Bale and Franck Ribery!

LEGENDS

2020

PULISIC

FACTFILE!

Age: 22

Club: Chelsea

Position: Winger

Value: £75 million

Country: USA

Footy Fact! In November 2018, Pulisic became the youngest footballer to captain the USA national team in a friendly v Italy - he was just 20 years and 63 days old. Wowzers!

100 PREMIER LEAGUE
GOALS CLUB

MATCH takes a closer look at the 29 net-busters who've scored a century of Premier League goals!

100 GOALS

Matthew Le Tissier

29

Teams: Southampton

Le Tiss was the first midfielder to bag a century of goals in the Premier League, and lots of them were screamers! His 100th strike was a typical stunner, spinning on the edge of the box to fire a half-volley into the top corner, and went down in history as the last-ever goal at Southampton's old stadium, The Dell. Legend!

Jamie Vardy

28

Teams: Leicester

When the 2019-20 season was put on hold due to Coronavirus, Vardy was stuck on 99 goals. But when it finally restarted he reached the milestone with a deadly double v Crystal Palace! The Prem's newest addition to the '100 Club' is still going strong in his 30s and, if he keeps up his recent red-hot form, he could move much higher up this list!

103 GOALS

Didier Drogba

27

104 GOALS

Teams: *Chelsea*

Drog had a massive impact on English footy. In nine seasons, he became the first African player to bag 100 Prem goals, broke the record for goals in both FA Cup finals and League Cup finals, and is one of only five players to finish as the Prem's outright top goalscorer in two different seasons!

Darren Bent

106 GOALS

26

Teams: *Ipswich, Charlton, Tottenham, Sunderland, Aston Villa, Fulham*

At his peak, Bent was one of the most in-demand players the Prem's ever seen! Tottenham, Sunderland and Aston Villa all smashed their transfer records to sign the pacy striker and, if you add up all his transfer fees, he's one of the most expensive English footballers of all time!

Paul Scholes

25

Teams: *Man. United*

As the Man. United fans used to sing, "He scores goals galore, he scores goals!" The Red Devils legend was prolific at the start of his career when he had the energy to fly into the box, but he was always capable of the spectacular – just check out his jaw-dropping volleys against Bradford and Aston Villa!

107 GOALS

Peter Crouch

24

Teams: *Aston Villa, Southampton, Liverpool, Portsmouth, Tottenham, Stoke*

Crouchy's one of the tallest players in Prem history, so it's no surprise he scored more headers than anybody else! He had plenty of ability with his feet though, too – he bagged a couple of wicked bicycle kicks, while his long-range volley for Stoke v Man. City was ridiculous!

108 GOALS

Ryan Giggs

23

Teams: *Man. United*

As well as smashing in over 100 Premier League goals, the Wales winger is also the only player to score in 21 different seasons and has a record 162 assists too. Mad!

109 GOALS

Emile Heskey

110 GOALS

22

Teams: *Leicester, Liverpool, Birmingham, Wigan, Aston Villa*

Heskey bullied defenders with his pace and power! In 2000-01, he helped fire Liverpool to three trophies in one season!

Dion Dublin

21

Teams: *Man. United, Coventry, Aston Villa*

Now a TV presenter and pundit, Dublin was so dominant in the penalty area that he was just as good playing centre-back as he was as a striker!

111 GOALS

Romelu Lukaku

19=

Teams: *West Brom, Everton, Man. United*

Romelu Lukaku was only 24 when he bagged his 100th Premier League goal, making him the youngest foreign player to reach the milestone!

113 GOALS

Ian Wright

19=

Teams: *Arsenal, West Ham*

Wrighty was a natural finisher and smashed in over 50 top-flight goals for Crystal Palace and Arsenal before the PL even began in 1992!

113 GOALS

Steven Gerrard

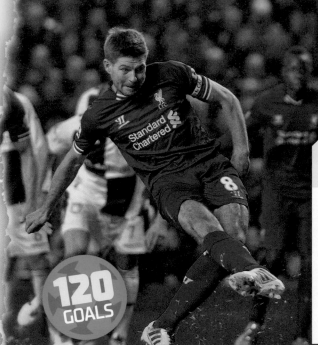

18

Teams: *Liverpool*

Gerrard is the best Prem player to never win the title, but the two times he came closest were also his top-scoring seasons. In 2008-09 he banged in 16 goals as a devastating No.10 behind striker Fernando Torres, then five years later he scored ten penalties as The Reds missed out on the title by two points!

120 GOALS

Dwight Yorke

17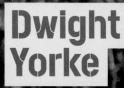

Teams: *Aston Villa, Man. United, Blackburn, Birmingham, Sunderland*

Although he scored most of his Premier League goals for Villa, Yorke will always be remembered as a Man. United legend. He was the club's top goalscorer during their famous treble-winning season of 1998-99, and formed a deadly partnership with fellow goal machine Andy Cole!

123 GOALS

Nicolas Anelka

16

Teams: *Arsenal, Liverpool, Man. City, Bolton, Chelsea, West Brom*

Anelka had spells in Spain, Italy, France and Turkey, but he always returned back to the Premier League. He was an explosive young talent at Arsenal and Liverpool, played a huge role in firing Man. City and Bolton to safety, then won a Golden Boot and a league title with Chelsea!

125 GOALS

Robbie Keane

126 GOALS

15 ⬜ Tottenham ▫️

Teams: *Coventry, Leeds, Tottenham, Liverpool, West Ham, Aston Villa*

Only two stars have scored more Prem goals for Spurs than Keane, and the club loved him so much, they signed him up twice! He'd been banging in goals for them for six years when Liverpool paid £19 million for him in 2008, but he quickly returned to North London the following January!

Jimmy Floyd Hasselbaink

14 🛡️ Chelsea ▬

Teams: *Leeds, Chelsea, Middlesbrough, Charlton*

We often talk about players with rocket shots, but not many could hit a ball as hard as Hasselbaink – he once struck a free-kick v Man. City that was clocked at over 140 miles an hour! He's one of only three players to win the Golden Boot with two different clubs – Leeds and Chelsea!

127 GOALS

Harry Kane

13 ⬜ Tottenham ⬜

Teams: *Tottenham*

In the last six years, nobody's scored more PL goals than Kane as he's built his reputation as both a Spurs legend and one of the most dangerous strikers in the world! In 2016 17, he won the Golden Boot with the best goals-to-game ratio in Prem history, and broke the record for goals in a calendar year in 2017!

143 GOALS

Robin van Persie

12 🛡️ Arsenal ▬

Teams: *Arsenal, Man. United*

For his first six years in England, RVP couldn't complete a season without getting injured. But when he stayed fit, he was unstoppable! Between 2011 and 2013 he didn't miss a single PL game and scored 56 goals, won back-to-back Golden Boots, and scored the goal that sealed Man. United's last league title!

144 GOALS

Teddy Sheringham

11

Teams: *Nott'm Forest, Tottenham, Man. United, Portsmouth, West Ham*

He won the first-ever PL Golden Boot at the start of his career, and ended it by becoming the Prem's oldest scorer aged 40!

146 GOALS

Les Ferdinand

10

Teams: *QPR, Newcastle, Tottenham, West Ham, Leicester, Bolton*

'Sir Les' was the main man behind Newcastle's epic 1995-96 season, scoring 25 goals as they threw away a 12-point lead!

149 GOALS

Michael Owen

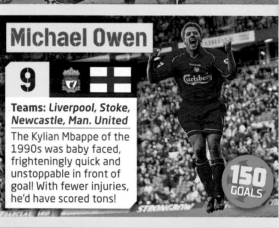

9

Teams: *Liverpool, Stoke, Newcastle, Man. United*

The Kylian Mbappe of the 1990s was baby faced, frighteningly quick and unstoppable in front of goal! With fewer injuries, he'd have scored tons!

150 GOALS

Jermain Defoe

8

Teams: *West Ham, Tottenham, Portsmouth, Sunderland, B'mouth*

In 2009, Defoe produced one of the most ruthless finishing displays the PL's ever seen when he hit five goals in one half v Wigan!

162 GOALS

Robbie Fowler

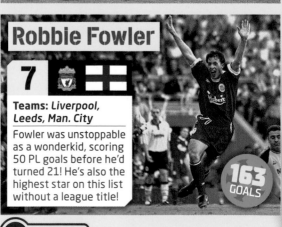

7

Teams: *Liverpool, Leeds, Man. City*

Fowler was unstoppable as a wonderkid, scoring 50 PL goals before he'd turned 21! He's also the highest star on this list without a league title!

163 GOALS

Thierry Henry

6

Teams: *Arsenal*

Very few players dominated the Prem like Henry did. He was the first player to score 20 goals in five seasons in a row, and the only one to win four Golden Boots! His blistering pace and frightening skills allowed him to create chances from anywhere, and he had the finishing ability to bury them. Total legend!

175 GOALS

Frank Lampard

5

Teams: *West Ham, Chelsea, Man. City*

Most midfielders are buzzing if they manage to score over ten league goals in one season, but Lampard did it ten years in a row! The Chelsea boss is the Prem's top-scoring midfielder because he was a master at timing his runs into the area, while also bagging a record 41 times from outside the box!

177 GOALS

Sergio Aguero

4

Teams: *Man. City*

You could argue that Aguero is the Prem's best goalscorer ever! The top-scoring foreign player in Premier League history has the best goals-to-game ratio of anyone on this list, has hit a record 12 hat-tricks and has bagged over 20 goals in six different seasons! He's sure to join the '200 Club' soon!

180 GOALS

Andy Cole

3 🛡️ 🏴󠁧󠁢󠁥󠁮󠁧󠁿

Teams: *Newcastle, Man. United, Blackburn, Fulham, Man. City, Portsmouth*

Cole was born to score goals! After joining Newcastle in 1993, he produced the greatest debut season in PL history by banging in 34 goals, and his brilliant form convinced Man. United to break the British transfer record to sign him. He then helped United win five league titles and the CL!

187 GOALS

Alan Shearer

260 GOALS

1 🛡️ 🏴󠁧󠁢󠁥󠁮󠁧󠁿

Teams: *Blackburn, Newcastle*

Shearer is remembered as a Newcastle hero, and rightly so – the legendary No.9 joined his boyhood club for a world-record fee and smashed their all-time scoring record! But at Blackburn he was unstoppable, too – he became the only player to bag 30+ Premier League goals three seasons in a row, and hit an all-time record of 34 to fire Rovers to the Prem title in 1994-95!

Wayne Rooney

2 🛡️ 🏴󠁧󠁢󠁥󠁮󠁧󠁿

Teams: *Everton, Man. United*

Rooney was destined for great things as soon as his first goal flew into the top corner, ending Arsenal's 30-game unbeaten PL run in October 2002. He never won a Golden Boot, but Wazza had way more to his game than just goalscoring – he's the only player in PL history with more than 200 goals and 100 assists!

208 GOALS

FREE DIGITAL PACKET!

Who's in your squad?

Open the Panini Premier League Adrenalyn XL app* and scan this QR code or enter the activation code to redeem your digital packet!

*Available in the app stores.

ADRENALYN XL ACTIVATION CODE
Expires 28/02/2021

1234-XXXX-1234

Enter Code or Scan QR

Scan the QR code with your smartphone to get a free digital packet...

Scan QR

...or enter the code manually:

Activate

PLAY AGAINST YOUR MATES!

Each packet includes six trading cards and one QR code leaflet, so make the most of the new Premier League season by not just collecting the cool cards, but also by playing online against anyone, anywhere in the world in the epic virtual game!

STARTER PACK!

Fans can kick-start their collection with an amazing starter pack! It includes a high-quality collector's binder, two-player gameboard and poster, 18 trading cards, a magazine game guide and two guaranteed Limited Edition cards!

INVINCIBLE!

INVINCIBLE

5

Keep your eyes peeled for this extra special INVINCIBLE card, too!

WIN!

OFFICIAL PREMIER LEAGUE ADRENALYN XL™ 2020/21 TRADING CARDS BUNDLE!

Thanks to our massive mates at Panini, one lucky MATCH reader will win four classic tins - each one a different colour with different limited edition cards to collect - and a huge box of packets... all worth over £100. Wow!

HOW TO ENTER THIS COMPETITION!

Visit... www.matchfootball.co.uk
Then click 'WIN' in the navigation bar on the MATCH website. Full T&Cs are available online.
Closing date: January 31, 2021.

A whole world of football is just waiting for you to join the game! Collect, play and trade your way to the top, but most of all, have fun collecting the stars of the Premier League! Visit paniniadrenalynpl.com for more info and get MATCH every week for ace Panini gifts!

MATCH flicks through the football history books to take a closer look at the greatest players of all time!

Marco van Basten
1982-1995

Country: Netherlands

Main Clubs: Ajax, AC Milan

GOAT Credentials: The best strikers score great goals on great occasions, and Marco did just that. In the Euro '88 final, he smashed in a sick volley from a crazy angle to fire Netherlands to their first and only trophy! That year he won his first of three Ballons d'Or, but his career was cut short by injury. He played his last game aged 28 with over 300 goals!

Ronaldo
1993-2011

Country: Brazil

Main Clubs: PSV, Barcelona, Inter, Real Madrid

GOAT Credentials: If you took CR7's power and shots, combined it with Messi's flair and dribbling, and threw in some of Neymar's tricks, you might get close to Ronaldo – at his peak he destroyed defences singlehandedly! In 2002 he fired Brazil to the World Cup with eight goals, and four years later broke the all-time scoring record! He was a 'Phenomenon'!

STRIKERS

Finally, the goal machines! These legends terrified defenders with their ability to hit the back of the net whenever they wanted!

Alfredo Di Stefano
1945-1966

Country: Argentina

Main Clubs: Real Madrid

GOAT Credentials: Alfredo Di Stefano starred in an era where footballers could play for multiple national teams. As a result, he represented Argentina, Colombia and Spain, yet never appeared at a World Cup! He made up for it in the European Cup, though – he was the main man in the Real side that won it five times in a row, scoring in every single final!

Pele
1956-1977

Country: Brazil

Main Clubs: Santos

GOAT Credentials: No conversation about the greatest players of all time is complete without Pele. He scored over 1,000 career goals, but his best moments came in Brazil's famous yellow shirt. When he was just 17 he fired Brazil to the World Cup by scoring a double in the final, and went on to lift the trophy two more times - no player in history has won it more!

HONOURABLE MENTIONS

Eusebio

Roberto Baggio

Romario

Thierry Henry

Gerd Muller

Ferenc Puskas

Dennis Bergkamp

Diego Maradona

1976-1997

Country: Argentina

Main Clubs: Argentinos Juniors, Boca Juniors, Barcelona, Napoli

GOAT Credentials: Both Argentina and Napoli have Maradona to thank for the greatest moments in their football history. No player has ever dominated a World Cup like he did in 1986, as he dragged less talented team-mates to the WC trophy with inspirational performances. He took that form into the following season as Napoli won their first-ever Serie A title thanks to him, and did so again three years later. What a player!

PRETENDERS

These stars will enter the GOAT conversation when they eventually retire!

Robert Lewandowski

Bayern Munich & Poland

Lewandowski's been prolific for the last decade - only two players have scored more Bundesliga goals, and only three have more in the Champions League!

Kylian Mbappe

PSG & France

Even if Mbappe retired this year he'd be remembered as a legend for firing France to the World Cup, but he's still got his whole career ahead of him!

Luis Suarez

Barcelona & Uruguay

Between 2010 and 2019, Uruguay's record scorer is the only player to have interrupted Messi and Ronaldo's domination of the European Golden Shoe!

Zlatan Ibrahimovic

AC Milan & Sweden

As well as being a ridiculous baller and an unstoppable goal machine, Zlatan's won tons of trophies and is still going strong in his late 30s! He's a freak of nature!

Sergio Aguero

Man. City & Argentina

Argentina hot-shot Aguero is already a Premier League legend as the top-scoring foreign player of all time, as well as being Man. City's record goascorer!

Wayne Rooney

Derby & England

As the record scorer for Man. United and England, Rooney is already in the record books as a legendary striker - although he's bossed it in midfield more recently!

TOPTEKKERS

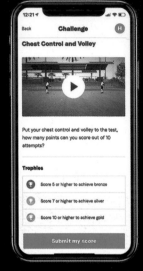

While football was locked down in 2020, MATCH teamed up with our massive mates at TOP TEKKERS to help you bust any boredom and keep your footy skills in tip-top shape! Here are our five favourite techniques to master...

1 CHEST CONTROL & VOLLEY

TOPTEKKERS' TIPS:

- Try to stay light on your toes and attempt to move your body in line with the ball.
- Move your shoulders back as you cushion the ball.
- Set the ball in front of your body with your touch.
- Volley it back with the inside of your foot, locking your ankle and pushing through the ball as you make contact.

THE CHALLENGE...

- Set up two squares made up of three large steps on each side.
- Ensure the squares are seven large steps from each other.
- Your partner throws you the ball from one square, while you receive it in the other.
- Score one point every time you control the ball on your chest and return it with a volley, without the ball bouncing.
- How many points can you score from ten attempts?

Chest Control and Volley

Put your chest control and volley to the test, how many points can you score out of 10 attempts?

Trophies

- Score 5 or higher to achieve bronze
- Score 7 or higher to achieve silver
- Score 10 or higher to achieve gold

Submit my score

5+ POINTS = BRONZE TROPHY   **7+ POINTS = SILVER TROPHY**   **10 POINTS = GOLD TROPHY**

2 TWO-TOUCH FINISHING

TOPTEKKERS' TIPS:

- Try to take your first touch into space.
- Strike the middle of the ball with your laces.
- Keep your head over the ball while striking.

THE CHALLENGE...

- Use a goal or lay down any objects that you can find as goalposts to use as your target.
- Set up a rectangular area roughly five large steps wide by four large steps long.
- Make sure that the area is approximately ten large steps from your goal or target.
- Place a marker one step inside each post, so that you have corners to aim your shots at.
- Grab a partner and ask them to pass you the ball while you're stood in the area. Take two touches, one to control the ball and the other to shoot!
- You have to make sure that you take your shot before the ball leaves your area.
- You have ten attempts in total - give yourself two points for goals scored in the corners and one point for goals scored down the middle!

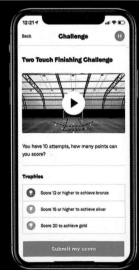

Two Touch Finishing Challenge

You have 10 attempts, how many points can you score?

Trophies

- Score 12 or higher to achieve bronze
- Score 16 or higher to achieve silver
- Score 20 to achieve gold

Submit my score

12+ POINTS = BRONZE TROPHY   **15+ POINTS = SILVER TROPHY**   **20 POINTS = GOLD TROPHY**

3 DRIBBLING

TOPTEKKERS' TIPS:

1. Take small, quick touches on the ball.

2. Make sure you use both of your feet.

3. Try to stay light on your toes.

4. Get your head up so that you can see what's ahead of you.

THE CHALLENGE...

1. Set up the challenge by placing seven cones or markers one large step apart.

2. Start at one end and dribble around all of the markers, then go back in the other direction, dribbling your way back to the beginning.

3. Ask a friend, parent or other family member to time you while you attempt the challenge.

4. How many seconds does it take you to complete?

10 SECONDS = BRONZE TROPHY

9 SECONDS = SILVER TROPHY

8 SECONDS = GOLD TROPHY

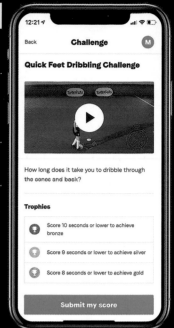

Quick Feet Dribbling Challenge

How long does it take you to dribble through the cones and back?

Trophies

- Score 10 seconds or lower to achieve bronze
- Score 9 seconds or lower to achieve silver
- Score 8 seconds or lower to achieve gold

Submit my score

---

4 THE CRUYFF TURN

TOPTEKKERS' TIPS:

1. Use your arms to disguise the move.

2. Get really low to the ground when you turn.

3. Plant your standing foot next to the ball.

4. Manoeuvre your strong foot around the front of the ball.

5. Use the inside of your foot to drag the ball through your legs.

6. Then, accelerate off into space!

THE CHALLENGE...

1. Set up a rectangular area roughly eight large steps long by four large steps wide.

2. Start at one end of the area, and dribble to the other.

3. When you get to the end of the area, perform the Cruyff Turn as quickly as possible.

4. Repeat the dribble and then Cruyff Turn at each end.

5. How many Cruyff Turns can you do in 30 seconds? Score one point for each turn you do!

5+ POINTS = BRONZE TROPHY

7+ POINTS = SILVER TROPHY

9+ POINTS = GOLD TROPHY

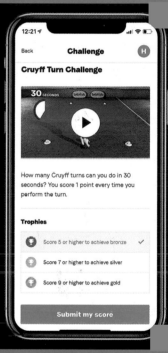

Cruyff Turn Challenge

How many Cruyff turns can you do in 30 seconds? You score 1 point every time you perform the turn.

Trophies

- Score 5 or higher to achieve bronze ✓
- Score 7 or higher to achieve silver
- Score 9 or higher to achieve gold

Submit my score

---

5 PASSING

TOPTEKKERS' TIPS:

1. Stay on your toes and move your feet.

2. As the ball comes towards you, step towards the ball.

3. Pass the ball with the inside of your foot and with your ankle locked.

4. Try to strike the middle of the ball.

TOPTEKKERS IS AVAILABLE ON IOS AND ANDROID.

THE CHALLENGE...

1. Set up a gate four large steps wide, with cones or any other objects that you have at home.

2. Make sure the gate is four large steps away from a wall or any rebound target.

3. Pass the ball from behind the gate to the target to score a point. You have 20 seconds to score as many points as possible.

4. The ball has to come straight back through the gate for it to be counted as a point. Go!

10+ POINTS = BRONZE TROPHY

15+ POINTS = SILVER TROPHY

20+ POINTS = GOLD TROPHY

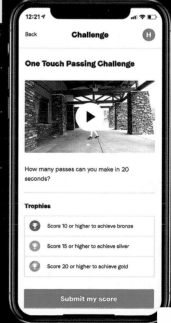

One Touch Passing Challenge

How many passes can you make in 20 seconds?

Trophies

- Score 10 or higher to achieve bronze
- Score 15 or higher to achieve silver
- Score 20 or higher to achieve gold

Submit my score

SUBSCRIBE TO MATCH! & GET THIS EPIC GIFT!*

COOL BOOMPODS SPEAKER WORTH £34.99!

PACKED EVERY WEEK WITH...

MASSIVE STARS

RED-HOT GEAR

STATS & FACTS

FIFA TIPS

PULLOUT POSTERS

PICS, QUIZZES & MORE!

SUBSCRIBE TO MATCH!...

CALL
01959 543 747
QUOTE: MATAN21

ONLINE
SHOP.KELSEY.
CO.UK/MATAN21

QUIZ ANSWERS!

Strikers Quiz — Pages 24-25

YouTube Star: Erling Haaland.

MATCH Maths: 9 + 10 = 19.

The Nickname Game: 1C; 2A; 3B; 4D.

Freaky Faces: Nahki Wells.

Grounded: San Siro.

Footy Mis-MATCH: See right.

Strikers Wordfit – See below — Page 26

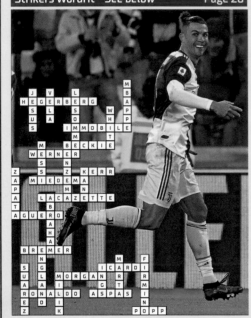

Midfielders Quiz — Pages 36-37

Game Changer: Marcos Llorente.

The Numbers Game: Three.

Odd One Out: Granit Xhaka.

Trophy Time: Jordan Nobbs.

Name The Nation: 1. USA; 2. France;
3. Germany; 4. Norway; 5. Netherlands; 6. Japan.

Mega Mash-Up: Miralem Pjanic.

Action Replay: 1. False; 2. Sporting;
3. More than £45 million; 4. True; 5. No.18;
6. 2025; 7. Wolves; 8. Watford; 9. True.

Midfielders Brain-Buster — Page 38

1. The Waiter; 2. Jill Scott; 3. Ajax; 4. Scotland;
5. Nike; 6. Georginio Wijnaldum; 7. True;
8. France; 9. Mauricio Pochettino; 10. Spain.

Defenders Quiz — Pages 58-59

Flashback: Leonardo Bonucci.

Steph Houghton Quiz: 1. Sunderland;
2. Two; 3. 2014; 4. SheBelieves Cup; 5. True.

Close-Up: 1. Virgil van Dijk; 2. Toby Alderweireld;
3. Yerry Mina; 4. Tyrone Mings.

Camera Shy:
Gerard Pique, Renan Lodi & Sergio Ramos.

Stadium Game: 1C; 2A; 3B; 4D.

Freaky Faces: Mats Hummels.

Super Skippers: Wolves - Conor Coady;
Newcastle - Jamaal Lascelles; Burnley
- Ben Mee; Man. United - Harry Maguire.

WSL Heroes: 1. Chelsea; 2. Man. City;

3. Arsenal; 4. Reading; 5. Tottenham;
6. Everton; 7. West Ham; 8. Man. United.

Crazy Kit: John Terry.

Defenders Wordsearch – See below — Page 60

Wonderkids Quiz — Pages 70-71

Footy At The Films: Lauren Hemp.

Spot The Ball: D9.

Guess The Winners:
1. Joao Felix; 2. Matthijs de Ligt;
3. Kylian Mbappe; 4. Renato Sanches.

Face in the Crowd: See left.

Wonderkids Crossword — Page 72

Across: 1. Forward; 4. Six; 6. Kosovo; 8. Saint-
Etienne; 11. Lauren; 15. Seventy seven; 17. Right;
18. Inter Milan; 19. Glasgow; 20. Hamburg.

Down: 2. Republic Of Ireland; 3. Bristol City;
5. Chelsea; 7. December; 9. Ten; 10. Barcelona;
12. Fulham; 13. Benfica; 14. Germany; 16. Nike.

One point for each correct answer!

SCORE /186